ESCAPE FROM SHANGHAI

Paul C. Huang

ISBN: 0615970745

ISBN 13: 9780615970745

Library of Congress Control Number: 2014903071

Contents

Prologue

World War II started on July 7, 1937 when Japan invaded China. Twenty-two days later, on July 29, Japan took Peking (Beijing). By November, they took Shanghai and in early December, they were in Nanking. The world watched the slaughter. The Japanese went through China faster than Germany through Europe.

By the fall of 1938, the Japanese army was headed south toward Canton. Fearful of another defeat, Generalissimo Chiang Kai-shek, the President and military commander of the Republic of China, ordered Governor Li Hanhun of Canton (Guangdong) Province to protect the gold bullion locked in the vaults of the Bank of Canton.

Facing certain defeat, Governor Li moved his Provincial headquarters from Canton to Shaoguan, a city roughly 175 miles to the north. He took the gold bullion with him for safekeeping.

This is the true story of how an educated, independent young woman joined the resistance, escaped from the clutches of the Japanese, and battled corruption at the highest levels of a male-dominated government.

Chapter One
Escape from Shanghai

As usual, my grandfather had gotten up early on Monday morning, December 8, and left for his office. Unaware that the world had literally changed overnight, his chauffeur turned a corner and drove the car into the hysteria and confusion on this street in Shanghai. Japanese soldiers were everywhere. They had already taken over all of the American banks and institutions, including the embassy. Out of his car window, my grandfather saw what he thought was a group of American men, women and children. He studied the faces and recognized a few of the men. Shocked by the sight, he wondered why they had been rounded up and herded together, shivering with cold and fear in the middle of this residential street. Clearly, they had been given scant time to pack or ready themselves. Most carried a suitcase or a hastily bundled bag of warm clothing slung over their shoulders. These people looked frightened, forlorn and bewildered by what had happened to them. A scared, tearful girl hugged a doll to her bosom.

The chauffeur slammed on his breaks. A Japanese soldier approached, inspecting the license plate as he walked menacingly at them. Kai Loh "Carlos" Sun rolled down his window and bowed subserviently. "Papers," the soldier demanded as he looked inside the Packard.

"This street is blocked. Go another way," he ordered as he returned Carlos Sun's papers.

The driver backed down the street. "Turn on the radio," Carlos said in a sad subdued voice, wondering what had happened.

The bombing of Pearl Harbor had taken place while Shanghai slept. Eight in the morning of December 7, 1941 at Pearl Harbor was 2:00 AM December 8 in Shanghai. The Japanese Occupation Army in Shanghai sat and waited patiently for daylight to attack the International Settlement of the city. This was the only portion of the city that they didn't already own because they weren't at war with the rest of the world. But that changed on December 7. The Empire of Japan had decided to attack the United States of America and at the same time, they also struck Hong Kong, Singapore, Malaya and the Philippines.

Clearly, the Japanese Army was sweeping across the International Settlement in Shanghai searching for and arresting American and British nationals.

Surprise and speed was their standard strategy. Everything was happening in double time. Carlos turned to take one last look out the back window of his car. He knew that his American friends had suddenly become non-entities. All of their valuable possessions—money, rings, cars, cameras, radios, house and furniture—had already been looted by the Japanese. Terrible things were going to happen to these poor frightened people, especially the children. He knew that many of them would die this winter in the Japanese concentration camps.

Sadly, he lowered his head as he listened to the radio. Carlos tried to focus on what he had to do. "Hurry," he said with anguish in his voice. He knew it wouldn't be long before the Japanese got to his house. Silently, he willed his driver to go faster knowing full well that the man was doing his best. Still, he urged the man on. "Hurry," he said again. Carlos trembled at the thought of what they might do to his five-year-old American-born grandson. A Chinese-American would give the Japanese a double incentive to be brutal and barbaric. Now that Japan was at war with America, the killing of a five-year-old American with a Chinese face would be full of symbolism for the Japanese. They could kill an American civilian because they could claim that this little boy was just a worthless and insignificant Chinese. After all, no one had stopped the massacre of 300,000 Chinese in Nanking in 1937.

They would be thumbing their noses at America by deliberately killing a Chinese who had happened to be born in America. The killing would be an insult to the Constitution of the United States. It would show that the Constitution was a weak and meaningless document.

The Japanese liked these subtle symbolic acts because it showed how smart and superior they were. This little island nation of Japan was racially pure, while the United States was a mongrel nation of mixed and inferior breeds. At that time, the anti-American frenzy among the Japanese was at its peak. Their daily propaganda broadcasts filled the air with hatred for anything American.

Jane Sun, Carlos' 29 year-old daughter, was listening to the same radio broadcast at home. Near panic, she rifled through her passport and visas looking for her son's American birth certificate. She hesitated for an instant, then brought all the papers to the charcoal brazier. Stoically, she watched the papers burn.

My mother was fearful for my life. I had been born in Ann Arbor, Michigan, which made me an American citizen. She knew what the Japanese were doing to the Americans—a five-year-old boy, separated from his mother, would not survive the brutal conditions of a Japanese concentration camp. She knew they would separate us because the Japanese had been ordered to take Americans living in Shanghai. My mother was Chinese.

At the time, I didn't know that I was an American citizen. My mother hadn't told me because she thought the concept of citizenship by birth was too complicated for her to explain and too abstract for me to understand. So she hastily destroyed our passports, visas and any documents that connected us to the United States.

Now, it would only be a matter of hours before the soldiers got to grandpa's house.

Three generations of the Sun family lived in grandpa's Shanghai brownstone. There was my grandfather and grandmother of course; Mom, their oldest daughter; my Third Aunt by marriage and her two children (her husband, my Third Uncle had died recently from blood-poisoning because he stepped on a rusty nail at a construction site. The Japanese couldn't spare the medicine to treat a Chinese. Third Uncle was an architect.); my Number Six and Seven Aunts; and my Eighth and Ninth Uncles: a total of eight adults and three children. (Growing up, I called my aunts and uncles by their family numbers. To this day, the only formal name I know is my Ninth Uncle's and that's because he emigrated to America.)

My grandfather knew the risk he was taking, but he didn't hesitate. After four years of living under Japanese rule, he knew the routine. He calmly gathered his family around him. "Japanese soldiers will be here soon. They are looking for Americans. There are no Americans here," he declared firmly. "We are a Chinese family. When they come, do not look at the soldiers. Lower your eyes, be deferential. Bow to them in the Japanese manner," he instructed. "If they decide to take anything, let them have it. Nothing is worth a life." Then he turned to his grandchildren: "Stay by your mothers' side and everything will be all right."

The family sat in silence, each person immersed in his own thoughts while waiting for the knock on the door. There was nothing else we could do. Talk would have been an useless waste of energy. In our own way, each one of us was mentally preparing ourselves for what's to come. Foreign observers often labeled this inscrutable behavior to be "the Chinese sense of inevitability," or "resignation to fate," while others called this "Chinese patience." I would call it the Chinese way. Even as a young child, I knew better than to act in a way that would make me lose face in front of the Japanese. I would not cry or show fear or give them any sense of satisfaction whatsoever. I would follow my grandfather's instructions to the letter.

What seemed like minutes later, fierce-looking soldiers with bayonets glistening on the ends of their rifles banged loudly on our door. They were doing a house-to-house search down our street. We lived at 131 Kashan Road, Shanghai, in the heart of the international concession.

Grandpa bowed subserviently and invited the soldiers in. Everyone was in the living room, including the servants.

"Here is my entire family. There are no Americans here. We are all Chinese," he said respectfully, hoping to save the officer some time as he calmly announced the obvious.

I hid behind Mom's cheongsam or Chinese dress. But I couldn't help sneaking a peek at those long fearsome bayonets. One quick peek at those sharp glistening points took all the courage out of me. Quickly, I retreated behind Mom's leg. I had seen the bayonets that skewered Chinese babies.

The fearsome-looking Japanese officer, with his long Samurai sword swinging from his waist, took a slow sweeping look at all of us. Seeing no white faces, he nodded his head in agreement with Grandpa's statement, then officiously turned on his heels and marched his men out the door. He had not bothered to check our papers. He was looking for blue eyes and blond hair, just as grandpa had expected. We had passed the first of many tests to come.

The Japanese hadn't connected my Chinese face with my citizenship. But my mother knew that eventually they would. A copy of my entry visa was at the American Embassy along with a record of my American citizenship.   It would only be a matter of time before they found my papers at the embassy. Then it would be all over. The question was how much time we had? The one positive note was that we had entered China in June 1937. The Japanese had nearly five years of paperwork to go through.   That could take weeks; it could take months; or it could escape them altogether.   But the Japanese bureaucrat was tenacious and thorough. We couldn't take a chance. It was now a race against time.

Mom had to find a way to get us out of Shanghai before they discovered my American citizenship. To protect the rest of his family, grandpa would send his children and grandchildren to live with relatives in the countryside.

The brutal and barbaric reputation that the Japanese had garnered at Nanking drove the family to take these unnatural risks. We had no choice but to flee. My mother was horrified by the thought of a bayonet through my belly.

⌒

I grew up listening to the reports of the atrocities that had been committed at the Rape of Nanking. I had a cousin who lived in the city at the time of the massacre. Ming and two of his best friends were out searching for potable water when he heard the marching boots of the Japanese. Instinctively he dove behind the rubble of what used to be a wall. He thought his friends were right behind him, but to his horror, they were not. They had been slow to react and a Japanese officer ordered them to stand where they were. His friends froze. The officer ordered them to drop to their knees and touch their foreheads to the ground in recognition of his power. His friends hesitated, unsure of what they should do. They looked at each with fear and bewilderment on their faces. When they didn't obey fast enough, the Japanese officer impatiently drew his Samurai sword and with two quick, precise strokes decapitated them. Then, without so much as a backward glance, the officer meticulously wiped the blood from his soiled blade with a blood-soaked cloth tied to his belt. Clearly, he had been prepared for the day's outing. Then he marched on haughtily as he sheathed his sword.

Ming knew that he had to escape this madness. He buried himself in a pile of dead, mostly headless bodies; some were still warm. The heavy warm smell of blood and death curdled his stomach but he fought hard to stay still and silent. He clasped both of his hands to his mouth to keep himself from retching. For several hours, he did not move. He would let the wave of soldiers wash over him. Once they had passed he would be able to make his way through their lines and out of hell.

When darkness came, he crawled from one mound of bodies to the next. There were so many bodies that the Chinese who had been forced to remove them could not keep up with the slaughter. Ming was able to cover a substantial distance while the Japanese soldiers were eating dinner and getting drunk on sake. He scurried from one pile of dead people to another like a rat in a sewer. Then he came across a series of dead, rotting bodies of school girls naked to the waist. They had probably been raped before they were killed. This abomination had been so terrifying that no one remained to bury the dead. This must have been the place where it all began, Ming thought. As if in confirmation, he suddenly broke into the relative quiet of the countryside almost as soon as he left the piles of victims behind.

He knew now he had gotten through the front lines. He was behind the attackers. Relieved, but still frightened to his bones, he decided to make his way to Shanghai. Ming deliberately stayed away from the banks of the Yangtze River because the Japanese used it to transport troops and supplies to Nanking. He stuck to the countryside, keeping the river to his left as a guide to Shanghai.

He ate grass until he came to a peasant's house. Thirsty from dehydration, he begged for water. The farmer obliged and he even gave him some cold rice. Ming survived because he was young and in good condition. But he had lost ten of his one hundred and thirty pounds during his ordeal.

When he reached the relative safety of Shanghai, all he could talk about was what the barbaric Japanese had done. He had heard that two Japanese officers held a contest to see which of them could behead one hundred Chinese first. (The Japanese newspapers published this account and even named the two men, not with condemnation, but with respect for their skill and zeal.) Ming knew that the Japanese paper's report was all too accurate; while he had not seen it take place, during his escape, he had seen row after row of severed heads lined up neatly on the side of a road.

And what was the justification for their barbarism? It was because the Chinese weren't worth the price of a bullet. What's more, we should be honored to die by the feel of the sacred Samurai swords against our necks. But the report that affected me the most was the one where the ordinary Japanese soldier tossed babies in the air and caught them on the ends of their bayonets. Like their leaders, soldiers held their own competitions, but not with Samurai swords. These enlisted men were not allowed to wield that sacred, ancient weapon. They had to use their modern-day bayonets.

But, decapitation wasn't quite as horrific as the sight of a sharp bayonet skewered into the belly of a baby.

How can any human being do these things?

"You know," my mother used to say, "the worst thing that could happen to us is that we die."

It was that simple and final. Death was the worst thing that could happen to us. Her statement defined the limit. I felt comforted, even reassured by her answer. In comparison with death, all else in life was insignificant. I grew up on this philosophy.

Still, I couldn't avoid constantly thinking about these horrors. Japanese atrocities continued to be discussed even at the dinner table. At grandpa's house, the men sat at one round dinner table while the women sat at another. We children sat at a miniature table and on chairs sized to suit our little bodies. Adult conversations flew around the large dining room and between the tables. The children heard everything, but we were not allowed to talk.

The adults no longer asked 'how could they do these things'—now, they just described what the Japanese had done in a matter-of-fact tone of voice. Incredulity was no more; one accepted the magnitude of the reality—this is who they are, and this is what they do.

The object lesson had been delivered at Nanking. Resistance was useless. The reign of terror had begun. In six short months, Japan had conquered nearly all of the industrial cities in China.

The Japanese had captured and occupied Shanghai in November, 1937. Then they marched inland to Nanking, the capital of the Republic of China, and carried out a policy of indiscriminate rape and murder that December. Sadly, most of the world didn't even know that Japan had massacred 300,000 people in that city—all within a six-week period. That's roughly 7,000 people killed each and every day for 42 days. Among those killed were young girls who had been gang raped then split open at the vagina with a bayonet.

What makes this 7,000 number so significant is that these were mostly individual, one-on-one killings with swords or bayonets. This means that during an eight-hour day, Japanese officers and soldiers were killing an average of 15 people per minute, or one every four seconds, non-stop, throughout Nanking for six weeks. These numbers sound unbelievably high, but when you consider the fact that 50,000 Japanese soldiers had participated in the Rape of Nanking, then that really works out to be six Chinese killed by each Japanese soldier during those horrendous six weeks—or one person killed each week by a Japanese.

Intellectually, I'm sure we will never know the actual death toll because nobody counted all of the dead. What's really appalling is not the numbers, but the fact that the Japanese could do these atrocious things to another human being.

But the real measure of hatred that the Japanese had, and perhaps still have, for the Chinese was reflected in the rapes against our women. These rapes weren't limited to young girls or pretty women; they raped and mutilated older women, too. One old woman had a stick shoved up her vagina and through her intestines. They left her to bleed to death. Their hatred was so profound that symbolically, the Japanese didn't want us to have the ability to reproduce, hence the stick in China's womb. And that the superior Japanese people should rule China because the worthless Chinese were clearly not capable of ruling themselves.

Ming told the story of his experiences with fear, passion and hatred—a near venomous diatribe that's never left my mind.

After the war, I found out that my cousin Ming had joined the Resistance and returned to Nanking. He had been haunted by the images of his friends being decapitated and it drove him mad. His blood was hot with the idea of killing as many Japanese as he possibly could. No one could stop him. One night, he slipped away and was never heard from again. (The Samurai sword was such a dreaded and hated weapon that General of the Army Douglas MacArthur ordered all of them confiscated and melted down. With one stroke, so to speak, MacArthur had destroyed the symbol of Japanese aggression.)

Meanwhile, in Southern China on October 1938, the Japanese had carved out a one-hundred-mile bulge out of the fertile Pearl River delta that included the port city of Canton (Guangzhou). Within this semi-circular bulge were the British colony of Hong Kong and the Portuguese colony of Macao. Many foreign countries owned a piece of China, but few people in the outside world knew much about it. (During a substantial part of the nineteenth and all of the twentieth centuries up to this point, China had ceded "concessions" to foreigners—pieces of territory essentially autonomous and run by American and European companies and bankers. Japan's invasion put an end to most of these concessions and colonies. After the war a few, like Hong Kong and Macao, would survive—but not for long. Hong Kong was the remnant that, by treaty, was returned to the control of the Peoples Republic of China in 1997.)

By the end of 1938, the fearsome Japanese had conquered nearly all of the industrial north of China, from Manchuria to Shanghai and Canton, a landmass that was over one thousand miles long and some three hundred miles wide. This is comparable to taking states from New York to Florida, as well as all of Pennsylvania, the Virginias, the Carolinas and Georgia—virtually the equivalent of the greater part of the east coast of the United States.

For us to escape from Shanghai, my mother and I would have to travel a thousand miles down the coast to Canton, then somehow make our way through the Japanese lines and into free China, some one-hundred-and-seventy-five miles north of that city.

Jane Sun (Ch'i Ying Sun), my mother, received her Bachelor of Sciences Degree from Yenching University on June 24, 1935. (Now Beijing University.) My father, K.P. Huang had also gradu- ated on that date. Mom and Dad were madly in love and they wanted to get married immediately. But, grandpa wouldn't approve of it. He wanted my mother to get her Masters Degree in America before anything else.

At grandpa's urging, my mother applied to the University of Michigan for a Master's Degree. She became one of the first Chinese women to be accepted to Michigan's graduate school.

Unbeknownst to my grandfather, Dad had also applied to Michigan. Mom and Dad had decided to circumvent grandpa's edict. They thought of them- selves as a modern, westernized couple. And in keep- ing with their desires, they had decided to elope. So in January 1936, they boarded the President Coolidge for San Francisco. A few days out to sea, Edward James, the shipboard Minister, married the young lovers.

On October 23, 1936, a healthy baby boy was delivered to the happy young couple at the University Hospital, Ann Arbor, Michigan.

Eight months later, in June 1937, the newly formed family of three returned to Shanghai for a two-week visit. At the end of those two weeks, Dad had to return to Michigan to complete his PhD. Mom, with grandma's urging, decided to stay in Shanghai a bit longer. She had no educational obligation to satisfy at Michigan. So we stayed, thinking that we'd go back to America later in the fall.

Dad left Shanghai for San Francisco in July of 1937.

Unfortunately, about a month later, on August 14, the Japanese attacked and bombed Shanghai. They blockaded the coast of China. No ships could either enter or leave Shanghai.

That's how my mother and I got stuck in Shanghai, and that's how Dad was separated from us by the Pacific Ocean for the duration of the war.

My mother knew how to read and write both Chinese and English. An educated bi-lingual person of either sex was unusual not only in China in 1941, but also in much of the rest of the world as well. After Pearl Harbor, her linguistic skills would become invaluable to both the Chinese and the American high command. Communication between the two countries would have been difficult, if not impossible, without people like my mother. Both she and grandpa knew it. They thought that one way to get us out of Shanghai was to immediately join the underground resistance. Their strategy was to get us out of Japanese-occupied territory and join up with the Chinese Army fighting in the southwestern portion of Free China.

Unfortunately, I was never able to get her to tell me the whole story of how she contacted and joined the underground movement. For some reason, and she wouldn't tell me what it was, she wanted to keep the process a secret. In any case, the details meant naming names and I wouldn't have a clue as to who was important and who wasn't. But, from the few hints that I got over the years, the process involved grandpa and his connections, both business and social. Generalissimo Chiang Kai-shek's Kuomintang Party had been financed by China's big businesses and wealthy families—especially those interested in keeping the Communists out of power. The only thing I am sure of is that grandpa paid a handsome fee to help things along, though Mom would not tell me how much. Discretion and humility was a great part of our lives. To boast of our good fortune would bring the wrath of the Jealous upon us. It was better to be humble than to gloat. That sounds old-fashioned, but those were the mores of the times. At least it was in my family.

Within six weeks, sometime in January 1942, the resistance delivered our forged travel documents, a new Chinese birth certificate for me, and steamship tickets. Because I was born in Michigan, the only way out for us was through deception. Now I was a real Chinese with a fake birth certificate. If we could escape to Canton and reach unoccupied territory, then Mom would have a job as the private secretary/translator to the Governor of Canton Province.

This was a rather important assignment considering that Canton Province has a land area of 69,400 square miles which is roughly equivalent to the land mass of New York, Connecticut and Massachusetts combined. When Generalissimo Chiang Kai-shek, the President of the Republic of China and the supreme military commander, realized that he was about to lose Canton, he reorganized the provincial government and appointed a new governor: Li Hanhun. Governor Li was also a General in Chiang Kai-shek's army. And, as part of Chiang's sweeping reorganization, the Generalissimo granted Governor-General Li the title of Chairman of the Kuomintang (Nationalist) Party in Canton Province.

These three titles gave absolute command and control of Canton Province to one man, Li Hanhun. Not only was Li the Commander-in-chief of the 35th

Army Group, but he also had the power to appoint the top civilian bureaucrats who headed up the departments of finance, taxation, education, communication, law enforcement, and the use of the political party apparatus.

And, most importantly, the Generalissimo had ordered his friend, the Governor-General and party leader, to protect the hoard of gold bullion in the Bank of Canton from the invading Japanese.

Obeying his orders, Governor-General Li moved his military headquarters, the civilian government, and the gold bullion to the city Shaoguan, the new wartime provincial capital.

Shaoguan is roughly 175 miles due north of Canton.

Now, all we had to do was to get there.

⌒

How do you prepare a five-year-old for an escape from Shanghai?

Mom began the process by telling me a story.

"Your great grandfather was the second boy of three sons in the family. His name was Sow Ping, or Little Soldier. That's right. That was his name. And you are the youngest soldier in China, too," she said with her usual smile.

"You see, Sow Ping was already eleven years old when he had to leave their small farm. The land couldn't produce enough food to feed three growing boys. Being the Number 2 son, he was the one chosen to go to the fishing village of Shanghai."

(For much of Shanghai's modern history, from the 1860's on, banks and trading companies from England, France, Germany, Russia, Japan and the United States had offices in the city. It has been argued that it was these trading companies that turned a small Chinese fishing village into an International commercial port. And their employees lived in the Foreign Concessions.)

"That's right, in those days, Shanghai was just a small seaside fishing village, not anything like what it is today. Well, Sow Ping and his parents had heard a lot of stories about Shanghai. You see, the foreign devils had sailed their big ships there, and the village was growing. He wanted to see those big foreign ships, and if Shanghai was growing, then maybe he could find a job. If necessary, he was willing to work for the foreign devils. He had heard that they paid well.

"To get him started in his new life, Sow Ping's mother tied a money belt around his waist. In the belt were two small gold coins. She hid the belt under his shirt and told him not to lose the money because that was all they could afford to give him. He had to live on those two gold coins until he found work.

"Sow Ping left his family knowing that his departure would help them have a better life. They would have more food because there was one less mouth to feed. With him gone, maybe the family could sell some of what they produced and make a profit. While Sow Ping didn't want to leave his family, he knew that it was his duty to do so. Like any dutiful boy, he left for Shanghai.

"Well, it took him two days of steady walking to get to Shanghai. By the time he got there, he had eaten all of the food that his mother had made for him.

"In those days, the heart of the old town of Shanghai was protected by a tall circular wall that was twenty feet thick. Oh yes," she said with a hint of awe in her voice. "Old Shanghai was a walled fortress! A deep moat surrounded the wall, and there were gates and bridges that could be raised whenever the Japanese Pirates attacked.

"Yes," she said with a sigh, "we have been defending ourselves against the Japanese since the beginning of time.

"Anyway, your great grandfather went directly to the market square. Farmers sold their rice and vegetables there. Fishmongers sold their catch. People could buy live chickens and pigs. Or you could go to the butcher to buy special cuts of meat. Prepared foods of all kinds were displayed and sold. There was a bookstall and a scribe for those who couldn't read or write. A pharmacy sold herbs and drugs. And there was a tent where traditional Chinese operas were performed and where magicians and acrobats showed their skills. But the most important thing to Sow Ping was the bank where the moneychanger worked. You see, it would not have been wise of him to use one of his gold coins just to buy some food. Showing the gold in public would only have attracted thieves. It would be much better to change the gold for coppers and use the coppers to buy what he needed.

"Well, Sow Ping found the bank and the moneychanger. The man was exactly where his father said he would be. He gave the moneychanger one of his coins. The old Mandarin hefted the coin, frowned with dismay but said nothing. 'Follow me,' the man said. He led Sow Ping through the bank and into the back courtyard where the foundry was. He held the coin between the tips of his thumb and index finger. 'This coin is a fake,' he announced.

"Sow Ping was shocked and dismayed. He couldn't believe his ears. He thought his life in Shanghai was over before it even started.

"'Here, let me show you,' the man said softly. He dropped the coin into a thick black metal ladle, then he placed the ladle on a hot bed of coals. He pumped the bellows with his foot and a sudden blast of heat and bright orange flames blazed against the bottom of the black ladle.

"Sow Ping watched as the thin film of gold melted away from the cast-iron core. The gold pooled into a tiny drop of molten metal, and next to it was the base-metal coin.

"'The gold is only worth a few coppers,' the Mandarin told him. 'I'm sorry, but this kind of thing happens all the time to you farmers.'

"Too shocked to respond, Sow Ping reached under his shirt and quickly removed the other coin from his belt. With trembling fingers he handed his last coin to the banker. He would be nearly penniless if this one turned out to be a fake, too. The Mandarin hefted the coin but this time, he smiled. He could tell by the feel that it was solid gold. Still, he didn't leave this to his skill or experience. He weighed the coin and gave Sow Ping his money.

"Relieved, Sow Ping left the bank. He felt lucky to have this money. He would have to double his efforts to find work.

"First, he went to every shop and home inside the old town, but the story was always the same. There were too many farmers from the countryside looking for work. The prolonged drought had affected everyone. But Sow Ping refused to give up. He left the walled town to search the surrounding area. After all, Shanghai had outgrown the old town. To save money, he ate one meal a day. At night, he slept in alleyways and doorways. And he always made sure that he got up before dawn so that no one could see him stealing a place to sleep.

"Well, one morning, Sow Ping woke up to the smell of cooking. Frightened that the owner would discover his trespass, he got up silently to steal away. But the odor of cooked food stopped him. He hadn't eaten in two days and his stomach overcame his fear of discovery. In the darkness of the night, he hadn't realized that he had chosen the doorway of a grocery to sleep in. And there, in the early morning light, he saw a broom leaning against the doorjamb.

"Instinctively, he grabbed the broom and began sweeping the front porch. After all, he had nothing else better to do. Worse, he had no place to go. So why not work? Once he started sweeping, he couldn't stop. Having been raised on a farm, work was a constant companion. If you wanted to eat, you worked. What's more, the physical activity made him feel good. In the past weeks, he had done nothing but knock on doors looking for work. Now that he's found it, he reveled in it. He enthusiastically swept the whole front of the grocery store.

"When he finished, the owner came out and thanked him. But even better than words of thanks, the grocer's pregnant wife offered him a bowl of congee for breakfast. (Congee is made with short grain white rice that's been steamed with water into a thick viscous rice-laden liquid. Then you can add your choice of diced pork; sliced fish; thin slices of beef; or small chucks of chicken. Some chefs add diced chunks of thousand-year-old preserved egg for additional body and taste. Cook with salt and pepper. Sprinkle some diced scallions and finely sliced ginger to the congee. Top off with liberal drops of sesame oil and you've concocted the typical Chinese breakfast.)

"After breakfast and without being asked, Sow Ping swept and cleaned the inside of the store, too!

"And that's how your great grandfather got into the grocery business. The grocer was expecting his first child and Sow Ping took over the chores of a very pregnant woman.

"He worked hard and saved his money. In time, he opened his own store. And since Shanghai was growing constantly, his business grew along with it. Over time, he bought land and built more grocery stores to serve a growing city. Now our family owns stores all over Shanghai. And it was all because of your great grandfather."

⌒⟶

It was cold when I woke up that morning. I could see my hot breath in the frozen air. The radiator felt like a chunk of ice. We had already used our small monthly allotment of coal. The fuel had been rationed to the civilian population ever since Japan attacked Shanghai. Sometimes, we didn't get any coal because the Japanese war machine took it all. This was one of those times. Mom used to put my clothing under the quilt to warm them before I put them on, otherwise it'd be like wearing sheets of ice. But today wasn't going to be like any other day.

Mom sat down on my bed to help warm my clothing. Then she carefully laid out a long canvas belt on my thick, fluffy down quilt. The seemingly weightless belt sank into the soft feathers. Slowly and with a bit of melodramatic hand movements, she unfolded the belt to reveal a series of small secret pockets. (If abracadabra were in the Chinese language, she probably would have used it.) Pretending to be a magician, she revealed a gold coin. Then with a flourish, a second one appeared. One after the other, coins, rings and diamonds glistened on the quilt.

"You are going to wear this money belt just like your great grandfather did," she said in a matter-of-fact way. Mom slid the canvas money belt under the quilt. It took a while to warm the gold coins.

An undershirt, a wool shirt, a sweater and a quilted down overcoat covered the money belt wrapped around my belly. My Sixth Aunt said that I looked like a ball of quilted down.

For a number of nights thereafter, I asked Mom to tell me great grandfather's story. I didn't tire of it. But, just as I had gotten used to wearing the money belt, Mom gave me another important assignment.

She showed me a neat roll of Japanese occupation money. "When we get on the ship, the soldiers are going to look us over. This is just something that they do. When they get to us, I want you to hand this to the soldier, OK? Just hand it to him. He'll be happy to get it.

"We're going to outwit the Japanese," she said confidently.

As a boost to my confidence, not only did she repeatedly tell me my great grandfather's story, but she told me this one as well:

"Once upon a time," Mom said sweetly, "there lived a woman who was about to have a child. She lived in terrible times. The land was poor and she was hungry all the time. She lived alone because her husband was away fighting in a war, you see.

"One day, a blind soothsayer stopped her on the street. The soothsayer put her hand on the woman's pregnant belly and said: 'You will give birth to a healthy, strong son. As a child, your son will slay a mighty beast. Dip your son in the beast's blood and he will forever be invincible.' Then the soothsayer disappeared as magically as she had appeared.

"Well, the woman gave birth to a boy, just as the soothsayer said she would. When he was a week old, he grabbed his mother's finger with his little hand. His grip hurt her finger! As he grew, she taught him to be gentle so that he would not hurt his own mother.

"A few years later, she and her son were walking near the woods. Suddenly, a giant, fire-breathing dragon stood in their way. But the mother was prepared. She took out a sword that she carried beneath her dress and gave it to her little boy. 'Here,' she told him, 'kill the dragon before he kills us.'

"The boy took the sword and with one mighty stroke, he slew the dragon! The dragon's blood flowed freely to the ground. Quickly, the mother grabbed her son by his right heel and dipped him into the pool of dragon's blood.

"After that nothing could hurt him. Not swords or arrows. The only place that he could be hurt was on the heel of his foot."

My mother as she looked in 1946.

31

My grandfather, Kai Loh "Carlos" Sun, was a slight, studious, bespectacled man with a subtle sense of humor and a quick wit. He was one of the first Chinese students to attend Cornell University, Class of 1909. He had arrived at Cornell in his traditional Mandarin robe and a three-foot-long queue down the middle of his back. He turned heads wherever he went on campus. Many Americans had never seen a Chinese man before. Especially one with long black hair braided down the middle of his back.

He had two roommates, both mid-westerners. There's a photograph of him flanked by two tall, hefty Americans. Both of them were about six inches taller than he. In his Mandarin robe, he looked almost like a woman standing between two men. Grandpa had the typical, thin-boned Asian build.

Once his roommates realized that grandpa had a sense of humor, they began to needle him about his braided pony tail, or queue.

His long hair was difficult to wash and even more difficult to braid. Back home, there was a servant dedicated to doing the men's hair. In America, he had to do it himself. And it took a long time to wash, dry and braid a three-foot-long queue. "Carlos, you're worse than a girl," they told him. They didn't know it, but this comment did not sit well with a man who came from a male-dominated society where women still had bound feet. Nevertheless the proverbial glove had been thrown down.

His roommates had also Anglicized my grandfather's name from Kai Loh to Carlos. They wanted to Americanize him and make him one of their own. But as much as grandpa wanted to fit in and be one of them, he couldn't do it.

"Under Chinese law, all Chinese men have to have a queue. You see, China was conquered by the Manchu Dynasty in 1644. The Manchu Emperor could not tell the difference between his Manchu officials and his Chinese officials. So, the Emperor decreed that under the pain of a beheading, all of his Chinese subjects must have a braided queue," he explained. But Grandpa knew that explanation sounded ancient. 1644 was well over a hundred years before the American Revolution.

Grandpa learned to love America and its Constitution. He had hoped that one day, China would become a democracy and adopt a version of the American Constitution. After all, both Cornell and his roommates had made a huge impact on him.

Here's what the Cornell Magazine wrote: "... Carlos Sun, of Shanghai, China, has been elected president of the Cornell Cosmopolitan Club. Mr. Sun is a senior in Sibley College. This is the first time that a Chinaman has been the head of the organization."

Grandpa had learned how to win a democratically run election.

Then, on November 15, 1908, the Empress Dowager Cixi died. The new Emperor, Puyi, was only two years old when he took the Dragon Throne. Grandpa figured that a corrupt and weak Manchu Dynasty could not survive without strong leadership, especially when the old-line Manchu officials were fighting among themselves for power and control.

More importantly, Dr. Sun Yat-sen, soon to be known as the George Washington of China, began to solicit financial and political support from America and other foreign nations to help him establish a democratic Republic of China.

It was then that grandpa went to the barber to cut off his queue.

His roommates were aghast and shocked by what he had done. They thought that he had risked his life because of their ribbing.

Proudly, grandpa ran his fingers through his short, American-styled hair. Then he told his roommates that it was time for China, and him, to enter the twentieth century.

A year after the Empress Dowager's death, grandpa graduated with a Mechanical Engineering degree. Here's what the Cornell Class Book of 1909 wrote about him:

"Kai Loh Carlos Sun, Shanghai, China.   Prep school: Cook Academy.   Univ. course, M.E. Years in Cornell: 4. 'Above all nations is humanity,' so above all the Cosmopolitan is 'Sun.' Adventurous, yet not rash, steady, yet not stagnant, fine-apparelled, yet not coquettish, good-mannered, yet not effeminate, he is everywhere Washingtoned by the gentlemen and Romeoed by the weaker sex. The glorious Sun is certainly not to desist from his work until every nook and corner of the globe has felt the light and warmth emanated luxuriantly from him. President of the Cosmopolitan Club."

By the time he got home, rebellion against the feeble dynastic regime was already happening. He fit right in with the rest of the young foreign-educated rebels. They had cut off their queues, too. They would no longer obey the Manchu Emperor even on pain of death.

The sight of an army of queue-less Chinese men made a stronger impression than slogans and chants. The old-line Manchu officials were shocked and outraged by this sight. But civil disobedience was here to stay. The rebels had made an irreversible stand. And they won.

In 1911, the Republic of China was born. Dr. Sun Yat-sen became the first president. (Though the president and my grandpa had the same surname of Sun, they were not related. But the similarity would play a significant role in our survival.)

Armed with his degree from Cornell, grandpa began work on building a modern China. He built railroads. He thought that the railway system in America was what made the country wealthy and great. And he wanted the same things for China.

My grandfather's study was almost a holy place that was forbidden to the third generation in his household. For a child to be asked to see him in his study was an awe-inspiring event. You would have had to done something unspeakably naughty to be called in front of him. In grandpa's house, it was up to the parents to discipline their children. That rule had never been broken. Still, I was shaken by his summons.

I've never been in his study before. In fact, none of his grandchildren had ever been summoned to appear before him in that room. I knew because I had asked.

Grandpa opened the door and motioned to the chair that was directly in front of his massive desk. I sat down while he ambled to his ornately carved, high-backed chair. He sat down and proceeded to talk to me as if I were an adult member of his family. From my position, I could just about see his head and shoulders. His desk was in my line-of-sight. It was both an intimidating and awe-inspiring moment.

"I have decided to send you and your mother to take care of our house in Canton. Shanghai is much too cold this time of year, don't you think?" he said with a smile. Nobody liked living in our house with no heat. "Taking care of our house is a very important job, you know," he said in a serious tone of voice. This had been the reason given on our travel applications to go to Canton. Then he leaned closer and whispered: "But what's more important is taking care of your mother. You take good care of her on your trip. You obey her. And be a good boy," he reminded me. "Always remember, you are my Number One Grandson, and the youngest soldier in China." He looked at me for a long time. This was the theme that he had repeatedly drummed into me. And every time he said it, pride swelled in my chest. I knew I was the youngest soldier in China because my grandfather had told me so.

Then he stood. "Come with me. I want to show you something." He turned to a door behind his chair and opened it. "I want to introduce you to your great grandfather," he said.

The room was dimly lit by two candles. The smell of incense hovered in the air. Thin lines of blue smoke curled up from the joss sticks. Two large portraits painted on silk hung majestically against one wall. My great grandfather and great grandmother's pictures occupied the entire wall. The light from the two candles flickered over their faces.

Grandpa lowered his voice and spoke in a reverential tone: "You were meant to follow your great grandfather's footsteps. Honor him. Never let the Japanese, or anyone outside of our family know what you are doing."

Like all Chinese children, I had been raised to listen and obey, and speak only when spoken to. And when your revered grandfather speaks to you in this way, what else can you do but nod affirmatively?

A. CAMMAN SULLIVAN, New York City. Prep school: De Witt Clinton High School. Age, 22. Univ. course, M. E. Years in Cornell, 4. "Sully" came from New York to "show us," but has been learning ever since. He took a course in Cross-Country for three years, but as the roads wouldn't wear out decided to rest and do reports for Sibley's benefit. We wish him good luck when he begins the long race in June. Varsity Cross-Country Squad (2) (3).

A. Camman Sullivan.

PHILIP ALOYSIUS SULLIVAN, Stockton, N. Y. Prep school: Fredonia Normal. Age, 26. Univ. course, Law. Years in Cornell, 3. Philip A. Sullivan, born November 8, 1882. They say for a November day there was plenty of hot air stirring at Stockton, N. Y., his birthplace. Fredonia Normal was his tutor, East Randolph High School where he first showed his great teaching ability, and now after victimizing the studes at Cornell for three years he is about to depart. Weep, ye heavens, weep. Phi Delta Phi, Chancery, Freshman Track Team, Toastmaster Freshman Banquet, Sophomore Banquet Committee, Toastmaster Junior Law Smoker, Alternate of the Intercollegiate Debate Teams, '86 Memorial Stage, President of the Law School Association. General Committee.

Philip A. Sullivan

KIA LOH CARLOS SUN, Shanghai, China. Prep school: Cook Academy. Univ. course, M. E. Years in Cornell, 4. "Above all nations is humanity," so above all the Cosmopolitan is "Sun." Adventurous, yet not rash, steady, yet not stagnant, fine-apparelled, yet not coquettish, good-mannered, yet not effeminate, he is everywhere Washingtoned by the gentlemen and Romeoed by the weaker sex. The glorious Sun is certainly not to desist from his work until every nook and corner of the globe has felt the light and warmth emanated luxuriantly from him. President of Cosmopolitan Club.

K. L. Carlos Sun

1909 Cornell Class Book

39

Grandpa took all three generations of his family to the Bund to see us off. He had deliberately hired eight rickshaws to take us to the coastal steamer because the number eight means good luck. The long line of rickshaws crossed the wide waterfront area along the Huangpo River known as the Bund. The one-hundred-fifty foot steamer sat by the famous Shanghai dock peacefully waiting for her passengers. Japanese soldiers had roped off the area by the ship. Three long tables had been setup with two inspectors standing behind each table. Half a dozen guards with bayonets affixed to their rifles made sure that the passengers remained in a neat and orderly line. By the time we got there the inspection process had already begun. Suitcases and trunks had already been opened on the tables and the khaki-uniformed inspectors were digging through peoples' belongings as if they were searching for treasure.

Grandpa, grandma, five uncles and aunts along with two young cousins came to see us off. It was a typical melee of a Chinese family saying goodbye. Exactly the image that grandpa wanted to show. He knew that the Japanese were watching. He wanted them to see us as a normal family with nothing to hide. The goodbyes were subdued but busy. Everyone wanted to say a few words to Mom and me so the jockeying of bodies looked like bees in a beehive.

Finally, grandpa knelt down, looked me eye to eye and said: "Remember: you are the youngest soldier in China." He smiled that gentle, good-humored smile of his as if this were just another ordinary day. Then he stood up and beckoned a waiting coolie. The goodbyes were officially over.

The coolie took our luggage and led us to the inspection tables. Mom took my hand and we followed. Her palm was damp.

The inspector reached out and said: "Papers."

He looked at the papers, then at us, then back to the papers again. The soldier nodded with disdain as if he were doing us a favor, then with a contemptuous look on his face he held out our papers. Mom had to bow and lean across the table to retrieve the papers from his fingertips. He smirked as he watched her bow to him.

The coolie put our suitcases on the table. He opened them and waited. The inspector shuffled through our belongings, deliberately messing up what had been neatly packed clothing. Then, with a dismissive wave of the back of his hand, he haughtily sent us on our way.

Mom rushed to tuck the disheveled clothing back into the suitcases. The coolie reached over to help. Quickly they stuffed the loose clothing inside the suitcases then hurriedly closed them. It would not have been politic to test the patience of this particular Japanese. You never know what might set him off.

The coolie once again took our baggage and led the way. He asked to see our tickets, found the cabin number then led us right to it. Mom paid him and he left. Interestingly, I have a vivid visual memory of the ship's cabin with its louvered doors and dark wood paneling. The events of that day still rolls through my mind like a movie.

We looked at each other thinking that the ordeal was over.

Just then, the loud speaker came on the air. The electrical voice ordered the passengers to line up on the promenade deck. Men in one line, women in another facing the men. Six feet separated the lines. "Don't worry," Mom said. "You stand in line with the men. I'll be right across from you."

She reached for my hand and put the roll of money in it. "You know what to do. Give it to the soldier when he gets to you," she said. Then we dutifully walked out onto the promenade deck and obediently lined up for the inspection. Unfortunately, when we lined up, I wasn't right across from Mom. There were more males than females, so the line for the women was shorter. Mom ended up being some fifteen feet away from where I stood. Mom nodded and smiled at me, mouthing that everything would be OK. I nodded silently in reply.

Suddenly, there was a commotion. A woman screamed. I leaned forward and saw a group of soldiers take a struggling couple away.

"Stand still," the man next to me volunteered. "The Japs do that just to see how the rest of us will react, so don't move."

Two officers casually sauntered down the line looking us over. One inspected the women, the other, the men. On they came. The soldier got to me, stopped and bent down to take a closer look. I was the only child on the ship.

Dutifully, I raised my hand and offered the money.

He smiled, took the money with one hand and patted the top of my head with the other, then he straightened and turned to the next person in line.

⟡

Years later, when we were reminiscing about the events of that day, I asked Mom whether she had been scared or nervous because I remembered feeling the dampness on her palm.

"Of course I was scared," she said. "But I knew we would come through it without any difficulties. You see, the Japanese have a very low opinion of us. It would never occur to them that a woman with a small child would dare disobey their rules. It would never occur to them that a little boy like you could do anything daring to outwit them."

Naturally, I was proud of what I had done. Mom made sure of that by praising me to the skies. But more important than pride was the feeling of accomplishment. I had accomplished what grandpa had told me to do. I was the youngest soldier in China. I kept my mouth shut to protect the secret I was hiding. And, most importantly, I was doing what my great grandfather had done when he left home.

I wore my money belt throughout the entire war.

Perhaps the most significant epiphany occurred when I got to college. In a Greek Mythology class, I realized that Mom had told me the story of Achilles. His only weakness was on his heel where his mother had to hold him to dip him in the River Styx—only I liked my mother's version better. Dipping him in the Dragon's blood sounded Asian and more exotic.

When I asked her why she chose to tell me this particular story, she replied: "What little boy wouldn't identify with Achilles' invincibility?"

Chapter Two
Canton

Canton is about a thousand miles south of Shanghai. Grandpa used to call Canton Province the "Florida of China." The family owned a winter home there. The house wasn't anything big or fancy, it was a utilitarian three-storied stucco located on the waterfront. Grandma used to go south during the cold winter months, but once the war started, she didn't want to leave grandpa's side. The family relied on our long-time caretaker to look after the property.

When we got to the house, Mom wasn't surprised that the storm shutters had been removed and that the windows had been opened. She reasoned that the caretaker must have prepared the house for our arrival. She opened the door, but suddenly stopped before she could take a half step. The room was packed with people. Men, women and children occupied nearly every inch of the first floor. They stopped whatever they were doing and turned to look at us. We looked back at them in astonishment.

"There's no more room here. Try upstairs," a man's voice said.

We went upstairs. All the rooms were occupied, even the hallways. We started to go up to the third floor but a fierce and angry-looking man glared down at us. "Try someplace else," he said gruffly.

"Come," Mom commanded as she grabbed my hand. We rushed out of the house. The squatters watched our every move with fearful, hostile eyes. (Canton had been occupied by the Japanese since October of 1938.)

"Mom, call the police," I said.

"Where would they go? The Japanese destroyed their homes. They have no place to live," she explained. "It wouldn't be right to send them away, now would it?"

"Where will we live?" I asked with fear and concern. We had planned to stay there until arrangements could be made to move us further inland to unoccupied territory.

Mom knelt down and took me by my shoulders. "It is not houses or money that makes you who you are," she said. "It is what you do with your life that matters. Do you understand? These people have no place to go. We do. I know you are scared, but try not to be. We will be all right, I promise you. We cannot throw these people out of our house."

Mom hired a rickshaw and headed for the water-front. Even though Canton was an occupied city, the Japanese allowed us to conduct life as normally as possible. Those who couldn't or wouldn't adjust to the new reality either left or died. There was no in-between. Perhaps the worst off were the displaced and homeless refugees with no jobs. The Japanese had not bothered to rebuild the homes that they had destroyed, nor did they try to create jobs. It made no difference to them whether the Chinese lived or died. All they cared about was taking the riches from the land. And in this part of the coun-try, it was rice.

"I hope our old caretaker is all right," Mom said. But she knew in her heart that he wasn't. (We never found out what happened to him.)

The rickshaw stopped in front of a massive, opu-lent, ornately decorated two-storied houseboat. Rows of Chinese-red columns supported the upper deck. Jade green shades protected the interior from the scorching sun. And intricately carved golden drag-ons swam along either side of the hull.

"This is where we're staying?" I asked in amazement.

"If they'll have us," Mom replied. Then she handed a slip of paper to the rickshaw driver. "Please deliver this," she said as she pointed at the houseboat.

The driver bowed and ran off to deliver the note. A few minutes later, an elegantly-dressed man in a white silk suit accompanied by a beautiful and elegant woman appeared on deck. She wore a light pink cheongsam speckled with little white flower buds. She looked so beautiful that I've not forgotten what she wore that day.

Two male servants trotted across the gangplank. They bowed, then took our two small suitcases.

Unconsciously, Mom looked down at her nondescript, peasant-looking dress, tugged at it to take out the wrinkles then smiled.

"Jane!" The woman in pink called out

"Oh, May! It's been such a long time," Mom said as she walked up to greet her.

"It's so good to see you. Welcome. Welcome! Please, please come aboard. But watch your step. The gangplank can be tricky."

Mom hugged May in a rare display of public affection. This just wasn't done in China, but these two were modern, western-educated women. They stood arm in arm like two long-lost sisters.

"And who is this, may I ask?" The man in white said as he bent down to gaze into my eyes.

"This is my son, Paul. And, this is your Uncle Jin and Auntie May."

They really weren't my aunt or uncle. Those were honorary titles for very good family friends.

"Come in, come in. Let's get you settled and we'll catch up," Jin said with a twinkle in his eyes. "Too many years have separated us. And so much has happened since," he said with a glance in my direction.

May and Jin were Mom's classmates at Yenching University in Peking (Now Beijing.).

Mom met K.P. Huang at about the same time that Jin started dating May. All four of them were in the class of 1935. The intelligentsia in the 1920's and 30's was trying hard to move away from the old ways and into the twentieth century. Arranged marriages were still the norm at that time, but it was permissible and "modern" for Mom and May to chaperone each other on dates and other social events. The four students became very close friends.

Jin and May married shortly after graduation. While K.P. had also proposed to my mother, grandpa didn't approve of the union. He wanted Mom to get her MS in Child Psychology first, especially since she had been admitted to Michigan. Her acceptance was a singular honor and grandpa didn't want anything to distract her from achieving her goal.

The four good friends went their separate ways. Because communication was so difficult in those good-old days, they lost touch. Now, after all these years, they had a lot of catching up to do.

"When father found out that I had been accepted to Michigan, he bought me a First Class ticket to America," Mom said. "What he didn't know was that K.P. had been accepted, too. We had applied together in secret, you see.

"I remember that it was a very cold day in January of 1936, when my mother, father, brothers and sisters saw me off on the S.S. President Coolidge. Father was so proud that I was following his footsteps by going to an American university. I really hated to deceive him, but I was so much in love that I didn't feel any sense of guilt at all. I was thrilled to know that K.P. was already on the ship waiting for me. I had arranged everything, you see," she said. "I even had him bring my wedding gown."

"Well, go on. Go on," May interjected. "Please don't keep me in suspense!"

"Once out to sea, the minister aboard ship married us. Oh, it was such a wonderful and romantic wedding!" Mom hugged me and squeezed me. I had heard this story before. "Nine months later, my beautiful boy was born."

"I knew you were going to do something like that. You were always the daring one among all the

Yenching girls! I would not have had the courage to elope," May gushed.

"Oh, I don't know about that," Jin added. "All of you girls were a bit modern. Maybe too modern," he said.

"Oh, don't listen to him, Jane."

"He may be right. I believe I'm the first in our group to have a child."

"Yes, yes, keep talking," May urged.

"Well, due to my pregnancy, I didn't finish my degree," Mom said with a hint of disappointment.

"Didn't you have an Amah to help you with the baby?" May asked.

"They don't have servants in America," Mom replied.

"Oh, of course," May said.

"It is difficult to raise a baby without servants."

"Did you do the cleaning, cooking and washing, too?" May continued.

"Yes. The American girls did it. They showed me how and they helped," Mom recalled fondly. "They used to laugh at me for not knowing how to do the simplest things."

"I wouldn't know what to do either, Jane."

"Anyway, K.P. had two more years in his Doctorate program, and I just couldn't wait two long years to see my parents. My elopement hurt them, I know that.

I really wanted to show my beautiful son to them. It wouldn't have been fair to keep their first grandson from them. So I decided to come home."

"Just the two of you?"

"No. All three of us came home. We came for a two-week visit. We arrived in Shanghai in June of 1937. He was eight months old," she said looking directly at me.

"All was forgiven once my parents saw him," Mom said. "But the astonishing part was that Bou Bou ("grandma" in the Shanghai dialect) thought that Paul looked exactly like her first born son. My older brother died at the age of one, you see. Bou Bou thought that this was a glorious omen. She doted over him like he was the reincarnation of her own son. She wouldn't let his Amah take care of him. And she couldn't bear the thought of our leaving in two short weeks."

"Well, I don't blame her, do you?" May said.

"No. Bou Bou convinced me to stay for a few more weeks. I didn't have to go back right away. We could follow later. But K.P. couldn't delay his return. He had to go back. So, K.P. left for the States in July as originally planned."

May and Jin looked at each significantly. "What bad timing," Jin said. They knew that on August 14, 1937, the Japanese bombed Shanghai. Their navy blockaded the coast. No ship could enter or leave China.

"So you were in Shanghai when the bombs fell," Jin said.

"Oh, yes," Mom answered. "We didn't have much warning. We barely got to the shelter before the bombs hit. They exploded one after another. The ground shook. We were nearly knocked off our seats from each explosion. One bomb came so close that the concussion caused blood to spurt from my baby's nose. Oh dear God, I didn't know what to do! All I could do was wipe the blood from his dear little face and hope for the best. He was only a baby. Just a baby.

"Then, suddenly the explosions stopped. The silence and stillness surprised me. I didn't think it would ever end. But it did, just as suddenly as it had begun.

"We had survived. When we emerged from the shelter, the family compound had been completely destroyed. Father had built it much too close to his beloved rail yards. Rail transport was one of their first targets in Shanghai, you see." (I was too young to remember much of that house. My only clear memory was grandpa's miniature steam locomotive towing two passenger cars and a caboose. Each passenger car had been designed to seat a child.

I remember sitting in the passenger seat while the train wove through the garden. Mom was never one to talk about her family's position or wealth. Consequently, I never pressed her for details because it just wasn't important. The net result was that I never knew how much real estate the family owned in Shanghai or how large a share grandpa owned in his railroad.)

"So, father moved us to our townhouse in the International section of Shanghai. And now, we're here," Mom said with a shrug. "Enough about us, tell me about you two. Where were you when they bombed us?"

"We were here. We were appalled to hear what Chiang Kai-shek had done to his own people. Is it true that he would not let anyone leave the city when the Japanese attacked?"

"Yes. Refugees were swarming to get out of the city. But his army blocked the roads and would not let them leave. The civilians were sacrificed to help defend Shanghai."

"But to no avail," Jin said with a hint of anger in his voice. "When they moved on to capture Nanking, I knew it would only be a matter of time before they came down here. If they were going to conquer the world, then they would need our rice to do it. I considered joining the army..."

"But I wouldn't let him," May interjected. "It would be a waste of his talents."

"Well, we discussed the situation. What could we do that would help our country fight the Japanese? That was a difficult question for us to answer. We knew that Chiang's Secret Service was more interested in spying on his political enemies than fighting the Japanese. So, we decided to create an informal organization of Yenching University graduates, a sort of alumni association, to help graduates with special skills fight the Japanese." Jin stopped and looked at May.

"The idea was simple. We're college graduates. Many of us are bi-lingual. We should use our brains, not our arms," May said, with some pride. "We spoke with our parents. Thank God they supported us. They preferred this to Jin becoming a foot soldier.

"So we decided to contact a few of our best friends and classmates. It was delicate at first because we didn't know the politics of some of the ones we contacted. We didn't run across anyone who sympathized with the Japanese. But, to protect ourselves, we decided to form cells. May would work with five trusted friends, and I would work with five trusted friends. And each of our friends would work with five others. We kept the group small. Everyone in the organization would only work with people that we knew personally. No strangers. And no outsiders. And then, all of a sudden, you came back into our lives!" May exclaimed.

"You two saved our lives," Mom said emotionally.

Both May and Jin came from wealthy families and both decided to devote their financial resources to fighting the Japanese. They had determined that only private funding could create a workable underground movement. They didn't want to be beholden to anyone or any political organization. In effect, their wealth allowed them to create their own intelligence operation. Only their mission was not spy on anyone, but to deliver the needed resources, both human and material, to the areas that needed it. This was how China worked at the time. Anyone with money could buy his own army. That's how "warlords" were made. Unfortunately, the line separating a warlord from one of Generalissimo Chiang Kai-shek's Generals depended on where you stood. The separation between legitimacy and illegitimacy wasn't a line at all, it was money.

Furthermore, it was clear that Chiang Kai-shek's government was incapable, both financially and philosophically, of supporting May and Jin's idealistic group of operatives. Instead, his secret police preferred to work with the Chinese criminal organizations known as the Triads. They raised money by trafficking in opium. Worse, Chiang lacked the will to cooperate with his own people to defeat the Japanese. The Generalissimo was always fearful of losing his hold on power. He feared and hated Mao and the Communists. Chiang fought a two-front war in his own country, Mao on one front and the Japanese on the other with the people of China in the middle. Ultimately, he lost on both fronts.

By the time the Japanese reached Canton, Jin had already established himself as a playboy whose main occupation was to smoke opium and throw lavish banquets. Even the conquering Japanese could not ignore his public persona. Naturally, Jin only invited the upper echelon to his elaborate banquets. And since he was apparently an apolitical party giver, in time, Jin's guests included high-ranking Japanese officials, both civilian and military.

Jin did his part right under the noses of the Japanese while living on his decadent-looking houseboat.

⌒

Since the time of Confucius, people lived and operated businesses from houseboats, sampans, junks and various other types of watercraft on the Pearl River delta. The size and design of which depended on the wealth of the individual or the nature of the waterborne business. A poor river fisherman lived and worked on a 15 foot sampan; ocean-going fishing vessels measuring 70 to 100 feet plied the sea; floating restaurants, some as long as 300 feet, fed hungry customers; shallow-draft barges that measured anywhere from 20 to 60 feet shipped rice, salt, wood, bamboo, hand-woven silks and a host of products to and from wherever the demand originated. Even during wartime, business flourished. The Japanese bought food and other products with occupation money. People took their paper because they still had a life to live.

Furthermore this vast alluvial plain grew multiple crops each year due to its temperate climate. The most important one was rice.

Three major rivers, the East (Dong) River, the North (Bei) River and the West (Xi) River, fed the Pearl River Delta like a three-pronged fork. A system of natural tributaries as well as man-made canals criss-crossed these flatlands. This interlacing waterborne highway system carried a wealth of goods from the interior of the country to the port cities of Canton and Hong Kong.

Historically the bulk of the opium trade during the 1840's took place here. When Great Britain defeated China in the Opium Wars (1856-1860), it acquired Hong Kong precisely because of this network of waterways. After all, Hong Kong sat at the mouth of the Pearl River where it flows into the South China Sea. From Hong Kong opium flooded its way up the three rivers to poison millions of people in the interior of China, while gold and silver flowed down the rivers into the British banks.

What happened to the civilized western nations that they would abandon all moral propriety to sell opium to the Chinese? The answer begins with Marco Polo. He found the Chinese living in unbelievable wealth. They wore silks; read printed books; ate from finely crafted porcelain plates; and drank tea out of delicate little teacups while the average European wore itchy, coarse wool, had no printed books, and ate from wooden bowls.

After several hundred years of countries like Britain buying Chinese silks, porcelain, and tea, the balance of trade was overwhelmingly in China's favor. What to do about this imbalance? Great Britain's answer was to sell opium grown in colonial India to the Chinese. By 1860, the surplus that China had accumulated over several hundred years of legitimate trade was gone. When the Empress Dowager Cixi died in 1908, China was effectively bankrupt, and it was because of the opium trade.

Now, the Japanese invaders had arrived, only their goal was not to sell opium, but to take China's rice. The Pearl River delta is one of the most fertile, rice-producing areas in China.

Uncle Jin's family fortune came from this vast, vibrant area. His family controlled and coordinated much of the commerce in the Delta. The family business connected the inland producers with the wholesalers in Hong Kong. Conversely, imported goods out of Hong Kong went inland through his network of shippers. His business dealt with hundreds of family-owned cargo junks. These cargo junks were the Chinese version of the independent truckers of today.

His job in the underground resistance was to send people and intelligence to the Chinese Armies fighting in the interior. Unfortunately, our sudden and unexpected appearance made life more complicated for Uncle Jin. We had been scheduled to live in Grandpa's Canton house to await Jin's call. Now, he was under pressure to get us out of Japanese-held territory. For security reasons, contact between underground agents was not allowed, unless, of course, they were on the same mission. But my mother had not been assigned to a group operation. She was to operate independently. Her job was to be the Private Secretary-American Liaison Officer for Governor-General Li Hanhun of Canton Province. (Or Quangdong Province. Or Guangzhou in pinyin. It's very confusing, that's why I've been using Canton, the original name for both the city and the province.)

Mom's job initially was to act as a translator-interpreter between General Chennault's famous Flying Tigers (a volunteer force of American fighter pilots) in his Kunming office as well as American Army Headquarters located in Chungking, the wartime Capital of China. She would be responsible for any and all English communications that arrived or left Governor-General Li's Office. More importantly, General Li thought that it would be more politic if his requests to the Americans for supplies and equipment were written in English rather than in Chinese. Li's Army had to acquire weapons, ammunition, gasoline and an untold variety of equipment to fight the war. And America was the only ally that could provide these supplies.

Thus, when Uncle Jin sent my mother's resume to the Governor, he immediately agreed to interview her.

Officially, Li Hanhun had multiple titles: 1938 to 1939, Deputy Commander in Chief 8th Army Group; 1938 to 1945, Chairman of the Government of Canton (Quangdong) Province; and 1939 to 1945 Commander in Chief 35th Army Group. And he was the Chairman of the Nationalist Party in Canton Province.

As decorated and as powerful as he was, Governor-General Li could neither read nor speak English. And he had no one on his staff who could communicate effectively with the Americans. There was an urgent need for a person with Mom's bi-lingual skills.

Uncle Jin quickly arranged transport for us to go to Shaoguan, the wartime capital of Canton Province where the governor had his headquarters. Li had moved his capital to Shaoguan in October 1938 when the Japanese took Canton.

Shaoguan was about one hundred and seventy-five miles, as the crow flies, north of Canton. But it was closer to 250 miles by boat up the winding rivers and canals. Most times, it would take two weeks to get a message up the North (Bei) River to Shaoguan and another three days to get a reply downstream. Given the time constraint, communication with Li's headquarters before our departure was impossible. And to complicate matters, his headquarters was repeatedly relocated to avoid Japanese bombing attacks. Governor-General Li was afraid of being assassinated by the Japanese.

Shaoguan was, after all, less than two hundred miles by air from the nearest Japanese airfield in Canton. The Japanese flew regular reconnaissance flights over the Shaoguan area, looking for

Chinese troop movements and General Li's field Headquarters. Consequently, Li didn't sit still. He would periodically and randomly move his tents, if not himself. He wanted to keep his personal location a secret. Few people knew his whereabouts, including Uncle Jin.

Uncle Jin could get us to the Shaoguan area, but after that it was up to us to find General Li, or he to find us. In either case, Jin would notify the general that we were on our way. And, he warned that there was always the chance that the message would not get through.

There were no modern means of communication between Uncle Jin and his contacts. Uncle Jin didn't have a radio. Messages were all delivered by trusted hands.

Luckily, we had a fall-back position. My paternal grandparents lived somewhere west of Shaoguan. We had the name of the small, riverside village (whose name Mom has long forgotten) and a description of the location of their house, but there were no maps to guide us. My mother expressed some concern about our ability to find the village, but Uncle Jin assured her that the local boatmen would know how to find it. In any case, we had no choice. We would have to depend on the locals. "The people who work the waterways will know how to get you there. Don't worry, we've been doing this for generations," Jin said with a confident smile.

Mom wasn't so sure. But she trusted Uncle Jin.

About a week into our stay, he handed us some well-worn and patched peasants' clothing. The disguise was meant to make us look like family members living on a cargo junk. Our role was to act like the daughter and grandson of the boat owner in case Japanese patrol boats stopped to question us.

Mom dressed me in what she called "my costume." We were going to live on a junk and pretend to be members of the Wu family.

At dawn one morning, a shallow-draft-cargo junk came slowly and silently alongside. The vessel was about forty-feet long with a ten-foot beam at its widest point. An overlapping series of semi-circular, woven-bamboo arches covered the cargo hold. These half-moon shaped bamboo roofs were rigid, waterproof and able to resist the strongest monsoon winds. There was a narrow foot-and-a-half-wide deck that ran fore and aft on both sides of the cargo hold.

Amidships, a section of the sliding bamboo roof opened. A crewman stepped out of the cargo hold onto the narrow deck. He wrapped one end of his rope to a cleat on the junk. When the junk came alongside the houseboat, he jumped aboard. He pulled on his line to bring both vessels together. When the opening in the junk lined up with a door in the houseboat, he tightened the line around a cleat on the houseboat and the slow-moving junk stopped.

The man looked up and down the river. No Japanese patrol boats in sight.

Mom and I had been hiding in the doorway waiting for this moment.

"Go," the crewman ordered.

She threw our two small bags to another crewman hidden under the covering. He held out his arms and beckoned me to him. I ran into his open arms. Mom quickly followed. The roof slid shut behind us. The boarding process took just a few seconds. We sat under the protective cover hoping that no one had seen us come aboard.

Meanwhile, in the stern of the junk, the owner made a big show of delivering a small canvas bag of salt. Uncle Jin thanked him and paid him as if this were a normal part of a routine business transaction. That done, the crewman unwrapped the line from the cleat and returned to the deck of the junk.

The cargo junk didn't have an engine or a sail. What it did have were the two narrow walkways on both sides of the vessel. To propel the boat, the crewmen would spear their twenty-foot-long-bamboo poles into the water until it found the river bottom, then they would put the front of their shoulders against the pole and push their way toward the stern. In this manner the men would push and walk the boat through the water.

When one crewman reached the stern, the second man would start his push from the bow. The returning crewman would raise his twenty-foot pole over his head in order to squeeze past the man pushing his way to the stern. The two men worked like a pair of well-choreographed dancers pushing their way endlessly back and forth. Two crewmen were assigned to each side of the boat. They worked in unison to make the boat go straight upstream.

This continuous process, where one man pushed to the stern while the other walked back to the bow, would repeat itself hour after hour throughout the day. The junk moved through the water at the speed of the crewmen's steps. It was a slow arduous job, but one that had been practiced for a few thousand years.

The owner, Mr. Wu, worked the tiller, always reading the river currents in search of the path of least resistance.

His junk had been divided into three sections. "These," he said slapping the flat of his palm on the hard sacks of salt "will be your beds. My wife and I sleep in the back, and the men sleep in the front. You will have privacy here." Our suitcases and bedding had been placed in the mid-section of the junk. The bags of salt were piled so high that there was barely enough room for an adult to crawl under the curved bamboo covering, but the height suited me just fine.

Our quarters measured six by eight, more than enough space for our makeshift beds and the few possessions that we had. Bamboo partitions separated us from the Wu's and the crew. And of course the half-moon shaped woven bamboo cover protected the salt, and us, from the wind and the rain.

The aft section was the center of life for the eight people on board. The space was only six-feet long but it ran the width of the junk. Here, Mrs. Wu cooked all of our meals in her brick-lined wood-burning stove. The stove was a compact efficient appliance with a 12-inch circular hole for the round-bottomed wok. Next to the wok were two smaller openings; one for steaming rice and the other for boiling water. Here, she made three meals a day. And boiled water for tea was always available. No one drank water from the river without first boiling it.

The stove and a small worktable had been built into the starboard side of the cabin, facing the shore. This location facilitated the loading of foodstuffs and firewood. The rest of the space was the living/sleeping area for the Wu's.

The Wu's cabin design was compact and utilitarian. Just enough sleeping room for two people. The removal of a few woven-bamboo panels opened the cabin to fresh air and the open sky.

Just behind the cabin was the narrow deck that Mr. Wu stood on to work the tiller.

The cargo occupied the entire hold of the boat up to the aft section.

There wasn't a toilet on board, and the only running water was over the side of the boat. Generally, we would use the toilet facilities on shore. These waterways have been used to transport agricultural and finished products since before the time of Christ. Consequently, all sorts of businesses lined the banks of the river to cater to the needs of the boat people. This included toilets and bathhouses. Significantly, human waste was collected and converted into fertilizer.

On one calm, quiet day when we were slowly moving up river, I suddenly felt the urgent need to move my bowels. There was no time to stop the junk or go ashore.

"Hang on to those two handles, lower your pants, then go," Mom instructed.

There were two vertical handrails built for this purpose, but they had been built for adults. They were spaced too far apart so I couldn't hold them and squat at the same time. My arms weren't long enough. I looked desperately at Mom for help.

"Just grab one and hold on tight," she instructed.

Mr. Wu stood nearby, watching with a bemused look on his face.

I grabbed a handrail with one hand and lowered my pants with the other, squatted down and my did business. That done, I took one hand off the handrail to pull up my pants. Only my pants wouldn't budge because I was still in a squatting position. I started to stand up to free my pants. The upward thrust of my legs put too much pressure on my hand. Unable to hold on, I dropped into the river. Luckily, the platform was only a foot above the water. I didn't have far to fall.

Mr. Wu let go of his tiller, took two steps, reached down and grabbed me by the hair. He saw what must have been a funny look on my face because when he pulled me aboard he threw his head back and laughed. Shocked and shivering from the chill in the air, seeing him laugh made me feel as if nothing out of the ordinary had happened. Wu handed me to my mother and asked his wife to give me some hot tea. Then he casually went back to work.

From that day on, Mom always made sure that I went to the bathroom on shore. After all, there was no speedy way to turn the junk around. If Mr. Wu hadn't caught me by my hair, then I probably would have drowned.

Mom taught me how to swim.

This was a story that the entire crew would tell, over and over, generating new laughter with each telling. Eventually, I took pride in the event. My misadventure had made them laugh.

⌒‿➔

Life aboard this transport junk never varied. Mrs. Wu would prepare breakfast at the first appearance of light. After breakfast, the crew would pole the junk up river for a few hours, then they would take a tea break and a short rest and return to work until lunch time. After eating, they napped or rested. Then a few more hours of work before afternoon tea. The crew worked until late afternoon when Mr. Wu would start looking for a suitable place to anchor for the night. Mrs. Wu would begin to prepare dinner.

At dinnertime, Mr. Wu anchored his junk alongside the muddy riverbank. To reach shore, two members of the crew dropped a long gangplank over the side. Then they would either drop anchor or tie the boat to a tree. Sometimes, they did both. The tough, muscular coolies wore faded and patched black pants and gray cotton shirts opened in front. They rolled their long, loose sleeves up to the elbows, exposing their dark muscular forearms. They would wash their hands and forearms in the river, chatting and joking, happy that the day's work was over. They were ready to eat.

Because the kitchen area was so compact and small, there was no room for everyone to sit and eat. We lined up in front of Mrs. Wu and she would fill a large bowl with food and hand it out to us. We would then find an available space, sit, and eat.

After dinner, the men smoked, drank tea and talked about the war. The commonality of the conflict brought everyone together. Once in a while, a crewman would go ashore and disappear behind some bushes. Urinating in the bushes was acceptable practice. Number Two was confined to outhouses that dotted the riverside.

By sunset, we would all be ready for bed.

At dawn, we woke to the soft chant of men poling the junk through the water. Here, the river ran between low banks along a relatively flat plane of land. It was broad and shallow with a slow current. Judging from the watermark of the bamboo poles, the river was about four feet deep. The beamy, shallow-draft hull was designed to resemble a flat-bottomed barge.

After a few days of poling, we left the heavily populated waterfront areas. Here, towns and villages were separated by towing paths that lined the river's banks. The crewmen stowed their poles and put on towing harnesses. They strapped them across their right shoulders then secured the ends of their harnesses to the long towline. The four men were tied to the end of this rope on shore. They were shirtless now, and they had rolled their pant legs up to their knees. Their hard thin dark bodies strained against the towline. Even though the three-inch wide harnesses were padded, the pressure cut into the right side of their necks and bodies. They pulled with their bodies leaning forward, nearly parallel to the ground. The men chanted to keep a steady rhythm. Their bare callused feet gripping the muddy shoreline with each measured step, they pulled the heavily laden junk up river.

The cluster of straining crewmen was about a hundred feet ahead of us. The long towline hung in the air behind them ending at the top of a fifteen-foot tall mast. This sturdy mast kept the towline high and dry, thus avoiding water resistance. Mr. Wu constantly worked the tiller against the slow-moving current. His job was to steer the junk away from shallow water since the force of the towline tended to pull the junk toward shore.

We moved up river one step at a time. Meanwhile, Uncle Wu was wondering aloud why we hadn't seen any Japanese patrol boats. Perhaps they were planning another invasion inland?

The way we moved up the waterways of China in 1942 hadn't changed since the beginning of Chinese history. Descriptions of junks being poled and towed on the eleven-hundred-mile Grand Canal date back as far as the Fifth Century B.C. For American-educated people like my Mom and grandpa, this continued use of ancient technology was exactly what they wanted changed. They had seen the future in America and they believed that modernizing China was the answer to the country's poverty and backwardness. One internal-combustion engine on the junk would have shortened our trip to a few days rather than weeks. But this meant a total reworking of the traditional ways of doing business. And nobody knew how to do that. Up until recently, of course. It took a violent revolution and an evolutionary forty years to make the changes.

One of the things that has always bothered Mom was the fact that we never quite knew where we were in our travels. We didn't have any maps and we couldn't buy any. When the Japanese invaded, maps of China were taken off the market and destroyed. The theory was that the invaders wouldn't know how to get anywhere. Of course the Japanese had made their own invasion maps, but we weren't going to make it easy for them.

So, we went wherever the Wu's took us. Consequently, I'll never be able to retrace our old route. At least not Mr. Wu's route.

What we were able to figure out was that we started our trip on the Pearl River, then we meandered across the Dongping Waterway, and up the Bei (North) River to Shaoguan. At Shaohuan, we turned left to the Wujiang River and up to my father's birthplace.

Mr. Wu had docked his junk at a market town earlier than usual that day. The announcement of his arrival brought out the local salt merchant. This was Mr. Wu's route, one that had been in his family for generations. His junk carried about 10,000 pounds of salt for sale and distribution along his territory. On his return trip, he would carry rice to Canton.

Wu's sons had been killed by the Japanese, so he knew that his business would die with him. He decided to devote the remainder of his life to fighting the Japanese. He was just one of many patriots who worked with Uncle Jin.

Over a cup of hot tea, the local salt merchant would bring him up-to-date on the latest news, then they would haggle over the price of salt. The two men sat and sipped tea. It was a slow, amicable process. They had been doing business together all of their adult lives. Each knew what the other's profit margin was so the haggling was more of a social ritual than a business transaction. After the crewmen unloaded the one-hundred-pound bags, Wu told them to take the afternoon off.

Mom and I went with Mrs. Wu to shop for food. We usually ate the fish that we caught in the river, but not today. On this day, she went to the butcher and bought a pork shoulder. She stewed the whole shoulder all afternoon. The meat was a special treat.

The next morning, we discovered why. First we heard the roar of the water, then, after we rounded a turn in the river, we saw our first white-water rapids.

There were three junk tied to the shore ahead of us. We became the fourth in line waiting to be towed. After we tied up, the crewmen on the first junk began to pole their junk to the middle and deepest part of the raging river. A two-hundred-foot long hawser was attached to its tall towing mast. On shore, a gang of thirty coolies strained their thin tight bodies against their harnesses, their left arms swinging with each step they took while their right hand pulled on the harness rope to help ease the pressure against their shoulders.

Though Mom knew that this method of transportation existed on the major rivers in China, she had not expected to see it here. Concerned and frightened at the same time, she asked Mr. Wu whether it might not be better for us to walk along the shore to help lighten the load.

He smiled at her suggestion. "Your weight makes little difference when compared to our cargo," he told her. "We will stay on board. It is safer. You will see," he smiled enigmatically.

Twenty minutes later, the first junk disappeared around a bend. Now the second junk in line poled it's way to the raging white water. Another gang of thirty coolies began towing the vessel up the rapids. Minutes later, we saw the first group of coolies return. They had delivered the first junk into the calm waters ahead and were on their way back to take the next one in line.

We were the last and the most heavily laden junk that morning so we had to wait for both gangs of coolies to tow us over the rapids. As we made the left turn into the bend of the river, we came to understand Mr. Wu's enigmatic smile. The coolies' towpath wasn't a path at all. They walked by the side of the river, ankle deep in water over rocks, stones and pebbles. Up until that point, the towpath was wide enough so that three to four men could pull side by side. This large cluster of men worked shoulder to shoulder and step by step up the onrushing water. But up ahead, the path narrowed. One by one, the men would detach his harness from the hawser then reattach it behind the man in front until all of the men were in single file, pulling in unison like a long line of well-choreographed men on the march.

We could not have walked in that rough, rock strewn riverside. What made it more dangerous was that nothing prevented the men from being pulled into the rapids other than their combined strengths of body and will.

I sat and watched the men haul us up the river. If just a few men faltered, it would have been over for all of us. But no one faltered or fumbled. They just plodded on and on, step after step.

By late afternoon, we came through the rapids into a broad, calm bowl-shaped lake. The dark-green waters were ringed on both banks by gentle sloping mountains. The scene looked like nature's hand had scooped out a handful of earth here and filled it with calm, dark water. The roar of the raging river was gone. The silence reinforced and accentuated the calm. Ahead was nothing but clear blue sky. It had taken us all day to travel just a few miles.

Further up river, we stopped at the foot of a gorge for the night before attempting to pass through the rapids. The sky was bright, light blue, with the hilltops on either side of the river crowned by the golden light of the sun. And down by the riverbank, a long dark shadow was climbing slowly up the mountainside at the speed of the setting sun, making the towing path a shadowless gray—and cool to the bottoms of my bare feet. The shoreline was dangerously rocky, paralleled by a smooth, well-worn, narrow footpath.

I had been bored sitting on a slow-moving junk all day so I decided to explore this beautiful shoreline. And as I rounded the bend of the footpath, I walked right into a band of river coolies. They were dressed in either faded-black or light-gray pants, rolled up to the knees. A few had gray shirts draped over their backs, but most of them were still bare-chested and hot from the day's work. The last boat of the day had passed through their gorge, and now they sat on their haunches, a huge bowl of rice in one hand and a pair of chopsticks in the other. The men sat in a near perfect circle around a pot of fish in brown gravy, a large dish of vegetables, a huge streaming bucket of soup, and a wooden bucket of steamed rice. They ate with gusto amidst a lot of loud chatter. Every now and then one or two of them would reach in to replenish their bowls with more vegetables, or fish, or both. They worked their chopsticks like miniature shovels, pushing and scooping the right amount of food to the edge of the bowl. Then they'd bring the bowl to their mouths and proceed to shovel the prearranged mixture into their mouths. They ate with unabashed slurping sounds as if they were sucking the food into their mouths. Eating was supposed to be an orally satisfying event, and they clearly relished it.

These men ate together and worked together. They depended and relied on each other for their survival. Mealtimes became occasions for them to express their gratitude at the passing of another hard-work day. The evening meal was a way to relax and celebrate their victory over the turbulent waters.

These men lived their lives by the river. They were here to tow junks. This hard-core group of men devoted their lives to this work. During the wet season when the river was particularly violent, additional men came looking for work. They were local farmers and town folks eager to make some extra money. Under normal weather conditions, the work was predictable and steady, as steady as the economy would allow.

On this white-water encounter, our junk got stuck on a rock. A call went out and dozens of farmers and laborers showed up to help. They did it with brute strength in numbers. Over fifty people worked in unison to help pull us off that stubborn point of granite.

And they didn't work for free. Every man who worked got paid by the gang foreman, who in turn was reimbursed by Mr. Wu. This was a negotiated fee. As for Mr. Wu, he would have to factor in the additional cost to the price of his salt at his next port of call.

At that time, China was an agrarian economy. Over 95% of the people worked the land. While farming is labor intensive, crops did not require constant attention. Once planted, a farmer had time to do other things. Consequently, they were more than happy to get an occasional bit of extra income by working the nearby waterway. This extra work was a long-standing tradition and the custom was passed from generation to generation. Some farmers looked forward to getting this extra income. At the same time, Mr. Wu and the rest of the merchants who depended on river commerce welcomed this practical and useful custom.

But, before we could go on, Mr. Wu tied a rope around his waist. His crewmen held the other end. Wu dove under the junk to inspect the hull. After a minute or two, his crew pulled him out of the rushing water. Wu took a few deep breaths and dove in once more. Finally, he came up for air and gave a thumbs-up sign. Mr. Wu declared that no damage had been done to the hull. And off we went.

As we got further inland, there was a section of the river where the water was so shallow that our cargo of salt had to be unloaded, then manually ported across this impassible section. As if out of nowhere, laborers would magically appear to do the work. Naturally, all of this had been pre-arranged. This was part of the rhythm of commerce along this waterway. Word had been passed from village to village. Peasants and day-laborers knew when we were coming and what work was available.

Being a supply-and-demand economy, the men's pay depended on how many of them showed up. More men meant less pay because the gang foreman had more people to negotiate with. Individual payments depended on how desperately you needed the extra money and whether you were willing to walk home empty handed. During good economic times, a healthy strong worker had some negotiating power. But not during the war.

Most of the workers who showed looked thin and malnourished. They were willing to work for a measly meal. And that's what they did.

Since there were more people than jobs, many went home with hungry stomachs and empty pockets. Much of business and commerce was conducted in this manner throughout China in those days.

Mr. Wu's and his coolies worked so hard and so consistently hour after hour, day after day that they functioned like a well-oiled machine. They were the engines that drove the junk, while Mrs. Wu provided the fuel.

They did this until they couldn't do it anymore. There was no such thing as retirement. If you didn't work, you didn't eat.

Chapter Three
Governor-General Li

By the time we got to Governor-General Li's capital city of Shaoguan in March of 1942, the battle lines between China and Japan had remained stable for almost four years. Japan controlled the coast and the shipping lanes, while China controlled the interior. The two enemies occasionally probed and punched at each other, but no major battles had been fought. Japan didn't have the necessary incentives to go further inland, at least not for the time being. And China was too weak militarily and politically to make a move to throw the Japanese into the sea. The status quo worked just fine for both sides.

Japan had every reason to be confident. China's steel-making abilities were practically non-existent. She couldn't make any tanks, machine guns, airplanes or artillery. And she could not receive any military supplies from America by sea. In fact, the only means for resupplying China were via the torturous, twisting Burma Road and by the limited number of planes that flew over the sky-high Himalayas.

Japan had a choke hold on China.

Governor-General Li's Army sat on a defensive battle line waiting and wondering where, when and how Japan would attack again. The attack on Pearl Harbor had everyone on edge. The people of Shaoguan knew that if an attack came, the Japanese would probably hit the provincial capital first.

Meanwhile, it was to Japan's advantage to keep the region stable so that people like the Wu's could do business almost as if no conflict existed between the two sides. When Mr. Wu met the salt merchant on the Shaoguan dock, the first question asked was about our trip: Were there any signs of an imminent attack?

"No way to tell," Wu replied. "Their patrol boats did not stop us, not even once. Perhaps they are too busy making preparations," he said with a shrug.

The tensions ashore were soon felt by all aboard the junk. The uncertainties were suddenly magnified. Adding to this tension was the fact that no one was absolutely certain where my paternal grandparents' village was. While Wu had made a few inquiries on shore, the answers were far from certain. Nevertheless, armed with a few meager facts, he turned west and sailed up the Wu River. (Wujiang)

Meanwhile, Mom's apprehensions grew. She couldn't understand how we could possibly locate a village without a map. She was tempted to get off at Shaoguan, but decided against disobeying orders. Not in the current tense atmosphere. It would be better for the Governor-General to find us. That way, he would know that we were not impostors.

"We are almost there," Mr. Wu reassured us.

A day later, he stopped at a nondescript dock and tied up. He seemed to know the men sitting on their haunches smoking cigarettes. Wu hopped ashore. He spoke with them, nodding happily as he listened to each reply.

Mom and I couldn't understand a word because they spoke a local dialect that we hadn't heard before.

"I have taken you as close as I can to your father-in-laws house," Wu told Mom. "His village is not far from here, but I cannot take you there. I'm very sorry. The water is too shallow. But this boatman knows the village. He will take you."

Mom looked around. The farmland looked all the same to her. "Are you sure?" she asked with some trepidation.

"Yes. This man knows the village," he said pointing at the boatman.

The boatman smiled and nodded confidently at us.

Mom looked uncomfortable and worried. The thought of being robbed, or worse, was ever present during these difficult times. Furthermore, she couldn't speak the dialect, so how would she communicate with the boatman?

Wu saw the concern on her face. Graciously, he raised his hands to his chest and placed his right fist in the palm of his left hand, then he bowed respectfully, showing both respect and humility. "You can trust this boatman. He will take you there. You have my word."

"Thank you, Uncle Wu," Mom replied graciously. She felt much better by his sincere gesture. "You have been wonderful to me and my son. We appreciate all that you've done for us." Then my mother started to reach for her purse.

Wu saw the motion and instantly raised both of his palms to stop her before she went any further. "No, no," he said shaking his head. "I have already been paid." He bowed respectfully once more. "Good luck to you and your son, Huang Tai tai," he said. "I wish you well, and may the River Gods be kind to you. Both my wife and I have been honored by your presence," Wu said and bowed once more.

The uneducated in China held the greatest respect and admiration for an educated person.

Especially someone who had studied in America. This fact alone inspired awe among Mr. Wu and his crew. Throughout our trip, they treated my mother with the utmost care and delicacy as if a special aura surrounded her that they could not or should not breach. They gave her privacy under circumstances where privacy was near impossible, yet they did it. I don't think any one of them ever came near enough to touch her. Nor did they ignore her as if she didn't exist. On the contrary, they respected her space and admired her position as if a princess were living among her beloved people.

Mom reached out to touch Wu on the arm, but didn't. She admired him and his crew for their fearless perseverance in the face of the river's raging powers. But more than that, she appreciated their ability to read and understand the nature of their surroundings without having to resort to books or maps. They knew things about the river that we would never be able to learn from anyone but those who lived and worked on these waters.

"Please Uncle Wu, you have been like a father to me and my son. You saved my son's life and I will never forget that. I am forever indebted to you. I want to thank you with all my heart."

Visibly moved, Uncle Wu bowed once again, then abruptly turned to address the boatman. Silently, as if he were too emotional to speak, he led us to the waiting sampan.

We felt sadness as we sat in the small sampan and watched as the boatman stood and worked his long, single-scull oar to and fro propelling us up river. We watched the Wu's junk move away until we couldn't see it anymore.

We never saw the Wu's again.

The boatman rowed us through a narrow tributary that connected the barge canal with the main body of the river. He pulled up to a well-made and maintained stone dock. Knowing that we didn't speak his dialect, he pointed and motioned for us to go ashore. He unloaded our two small bags and held the boat steady as Mom and I got off. My mother paid him and away he rowed, leaving us standing forlornly at the dock.

There was no one in sight. A narrow one-lane dirt road ran by the public dock. We climbed the three steps up to the road to get a better idea of our location. Still no sight of a human being. To our right was a stone warehouse and next to that was a two-story merchant's house. That was it. There was no town center or even a village. We hadn't expected such a desolate and remote location. Concerned, Mom quickly turned to call to the boatman, but he was already beyond shouting distance.

Quickly, Mom reached into her purse and removed the letter. She unfolded it with nervous fingers, her eyes darting down the page looking for the directions. Relieved, she pointed to her left and said: "There!" she pointed. "The house should be over there," she said with some uncertainty.

We walked down the road about a quarter of a mile. She glanced at the letter again. "This must be it," she said as she pointed at the long windowless wall of a traditional compound. "Come on, this way," she commanded as she took my hand. Her palm was wet.

We stopped in front of the main entrance and looked up at the sign over the arched doorway. "This is it," she announced with a sigh of relief. "This is where your father was born."

Again, Uncle Jin had done his job. Mom's letter informing my grandparents of our imminent arrival had found its destination the old fashion way. All Jin needed was the Huang name and the name of the village and the message got through. It was miraculous.

⌒

The main entrance of the Huang compound faced south because the river ran north to south. The west wall fronted on the river while the east wall faced Grandfather Huang's farmland. There were no windows on any of the walls. The only openings were the front entrance and the back door, both of which were located in the exact centers of their respective walls. This design was in accordance with the tradition of fung-sui (spelling in Cantonese), literally translated as "wind-water."

Should the river ever flood, they would open the back door to let the water run through the compound and out the front door, thus creating the line of least water resistance. This was one of the most fundamental aspects of the origin of the art of fung-sui. Don't fight nature if you know what's good for you. A pliable stick bends with the wind, a rigid one breaks.

We stood under a peaked, six-foot section of green-tiled roof that protected both the front door and the visitor from the sun and rain. Hung squarely in the center of the door was a faded red, rectangular wooden plaque with the family name inscribed in black ink. Mom knocked. We waited. Then she knocked again. And we waited some more. Mom stepped back and looked at the sign above the door to reassure herself. Then she knocked again.

"Coming!" shouted a deep gruff voice. "I told you I heard knocking!"

Suddenly, the door swung open and an elderly white-haired man looked down at us. He turned his head and shouted over his left shoulder: "They're here!"

A few feet behind him stood a short, chubby gray-haired women dressed in a gray peasant's cheongsam. She wore a pair of gray cloth shoes, ones that she had made for herself from an old discarded dress. She would cut the cloth to match the size and shape of her foot, and then sew a dozen or more of these patterns together to make the sole. Then she would sew a cover for the arch of her foot and her toes and that was it. A pair of cloth slippers that she would use in place of shoes. But most times, she went barefoot.

She had peasant's feet, that is, they were unbroken and unbound. In the old days, people who had pretensions to wealth and ambitions for social status broke their young daughter's feet at the arch and folded the girl's toes under her foot. Then the foot was bound so tightly that the bones wouldn't grow. These girls would grow up to have tiny little feet, no more than four inches long. And they would, in effect, be walking on the tops of their toes. By wearing a long cheongsam that touched the floor, it would appear that these ladies were gliding on a cushion of air, when in reality, they were taking tiny little quick steps like a ballerina.

This painful procedure was supposed to make the women sexy looking as they seemingly floated by.

Grandma was overweight and proud of it. This was a sign of prosperity. She wasn't living from meal to meal like a poor peasant. She had plenty to eat and plenty of rice in storage.

"Do you speak Cantonese?" Grandfather Huang asked in his local version of the dialect.

Mother shook her head. "A little bit," she replied to be polite. But the truth was that she understood just enough to get by. (Mom spoke the Shanghai dialect where she was born, and she learned the Mandarin dialect when she went to Yenching University in Peking. To the "ungifted" ear, all the Chinese regional dialects sounded like a foreign language. I grew up speaking the Shanghai dialect, but I eventually learned Cantonese.)

"Ah," grandfather said. Silently, awkwardly, he led the way. The entryway was about fifteen feet wide and twenty feet deep. Gray brick walls towered over us on both sides. There were two windows in each of these walls, but the wooden shutters were closed.

Grandfather Huang's walled-in riverfront compound was about fifty feet wide and eighty feet deep. Adjacent to both sides of the front entrance was the main living quarters for my grandparents. The single-story house on the right was their personal living quarters. The one on the left was the main room where guests were entertained.

Built against the riverfront wall was a long one-story structure that housed three bedrooms. Mom and I lived in the one that was farthest from the Main room. Our bedroom was square, with a hard dirt floor, two single beds, one chair and a small writing table.

The windowless back wall of our room faced the river. Like the Great Wall of China, this design was meant to keep people out, both visually and physically. The door faced the interior courtyard. Two sash-less square windows flanked the door. Wooden shutters hung on either side of them.

Across the open interior garden stood three rooms that were used as the kitchen, dining room and grandfather's workroom. The kitchen was in the center with a well in front. The dining room was to the right of it, and outside, in front of the dining room was a large, wooden table. We could have our meals alfresco, too. The compound was situated so that we ate dinner in the shade of the late afternoon sun.

By Chinese standards, this was a middle-class landowner's house. In truth, there were only two classes of people out here: the landowners and the peasant/sharecroppers. And due to its fortress-like architecture, the family was inward-looking, self-contained and unaffected by outside influences. This structure also protected the occupants from bandits who might otherwise want to steal their store of rice.

Most Chinese peasants eat rice three times a day, or about one pound per person per day. In China, the word for food is rice. "Have you eaten rice yet?" means "have you eaten yet?" And the time when that question is asked would define the meal. That question at 6 PM would mean have you had dinner yet. The same goes for breakfast and lunch.

Grandpa had two thousand pounds of rice stored in his secret emergency rice bin. That was probably sufficient to survive a two-year drought. This store did not include their normal, everyday supply. Most peasants would be lucky to have a six months supply to carry them through the winter. For most peasants in China, it was a hand-to-mouth subsistence lifestyle. They lived on what they produced. And if you had a year or two of reserves, you considered yourself lucky and fortunate, wealthy even, especially if you have a surplus to sell.

There were two outhouses about thirty feet from our living quarters near the rear wall. The outhouses were hidden by trees and bushes and they were as far away from the well as they could possibly be, a safe distance of 70 feet. This distance ensured a safe and uncontaminated water supply. Nevertheless, water was always boiled before drinking. Once the ancient

wise men connected sickness and disease with con-
taminated and unclean water, the tea ceremony was
created to promote boiling water before drinking.
What started out to be health issue turned into a
social ceremony. Everybody drinks tea or just plain
hot water.

Before our arrival, my grandparents were the only
ones living there. All of their grown children had
left. No one in the family wanted to continue farming. It was hard, boring work with a limited future.
The only thing you had to look forward to was more
of the same—year after year until you died. My father
had taken the competitive exams and scored high
enough to get into Yenching University. He would
never return.

In this part of rural China, the biggest building
in the village was the warehouse where the grain was
stored. Next to this stone building was the grain
merchant's house. His house was the center of the
village. From here, the merchant could ship the
grain grown by the surrounding farmers throughout
China. (More likely than not, through Jin's shipping
network.)

There were no stores here or a village center simply because the people lived on their self-contained
farms. They produced what they needed. And what
they didn't produce, they traded with friends and

neighbors. Thus, the farm houses were scattered hither and yon, a few on the river, but mostly inland. Most peasant farmers in the area lived in small one to two room houses. Many of these farmers leased land from my grandfather.

The biggest public facility was the village elementary school, which was up river about a half mile beyond my grandfather's compound. The school system here was rudimentary. It was a public/private organization; the government provided the facilities and a basic annual salary to the teacher. When I was there, we had a teacher and an assistant to care for thirty children in a one-room schoolhouse. The number of teachers during any given year would depend on enrollment.

The private aspect of the system was this: according to Confucian tradition, it was the teacher's duty to discover, encourage and promote students with above-average potential. In my father's day, his teacher recognized his potential and thought that he was university material. Once this potential was made known to my grandfather, then it was his duty to hire the teacher to cultivate my father's potential. The teacher would tutor my father in the classics and calligraphy to pass the various exams.

A good teacher, like Confucius himself, would spend his professional life teaching others to achieve greatness. Great teachers were selfless men intent on forwarding the careers of others. But like all human endeavors, not all teachers are selfless. Nevertheless, teaching was and still is a respected and admired profession in China. A renowned teacher could make a decent living. In this ideal system, the teacher, the student and society in general benefited.

Grandfather Huang was a taciturn man accustomed to delivering short directives and commands to his wife. Aside from ordering food and asking for more tea, he did not talk to her. The talk, mostly about nothing in particular, was generated by my grandmother. And she talked incessantly, stopping only when she was putting food into her mouth but commencing once more even while chewing. She had a captive audience at mealtimes, and she was not about to waste her opportunity to exercise her vocabulary. But, the moment my grandfather started to speak, she would instantly fall silent. And he didn't talk very often.

Since neither Mom nor I understood their local dialect, talking was not an easy pastime. Communication was through hand gestures supported by an occasional word or two.

Most of the time, grandfather would disappear into his workroom. He came out at mealtimes. He referred to her as his "Low Pau" or "Old Wife" in peasant Cantonese. It was a derogatory and uncouth term used by the coarsest of peasants. She was not allowed into his workroom.

Initially, Mom winced whenever she heard "Low Pau", but after the first few days, she got used to it. To avoid any in-law unpleasantness, we generally stayed in our room, exiting only when grandma called us to eat.

This was the first time that Mom had met her in-laws. And it was clear to the both of us that my grandmother was more of a servant than a wife. She was ignored and treated in an off-handed, dismissive manner. It was unpleasant and awkward to watch.

A few days later, I heard an airplane flying over-head. I ran out into the middle of the courtyard scanning the sky for the source of the sound. At the time, just seeing an airplane in the sky was an earth-shaking event. I knew that this was a Japanese reconnaissance plane that made regularly sched-uled flights over Chinese territory. During our trip upriver, we saw these planes regularly. They followed a predictable and rigid schedule. The flights were meant to spy on Chinese troop movements and to instill fear and intimidation. But before I could spot the plane, I felt an arm grab me around the waist, pluck me off the ground and carried me on the run into the kitchen. As she ran, my grandmother kept uttering a constant stream of tearful and fearful gibberish that I did not understand. Before I could react, she dove under the kitchen table and smothered me with her body. What frightened me was not the airplane, but her unexpected actions and uncontrollable fear. I struggled to get free, but by that time, the plane was gone.

Afterwards, I described the guttural sounds that she made and asked Mom what it all meant. "She was probably praying to the Gods to protect us from harm."

"But the plane never drops bombs."

"Yes, but she doesn't know that. This is where she's lived most of her life. She's uneducated, illiterate and superstitious. She doesn't know what an airplane is. She thinks it's some kind of black magic that the Japanese have harnessed. She is deathly afraid of the terror that these planes can rain down on her. You really can't blame her.

"The missionaries have done a good job converting your Grandmother into a Christian. She mixes western religion with Buddhism and ancient Chinese Superstitions to create a magical prayer that keeps the bombs from falling on her house. She is just ignorant and superstitious, that's all. It's best to stay away from her," Mom said.

The best hiding place was in my grandfather's workroom. His room was really a warehouse. Stacks of bamboo baskets of all sizes and shapes stood from floor to ceiling and wall to wall. There were twelve-inch steamers for the home-sized wok and twenty-four and thirty-six-inch ones for commercial use. He was too old now to do actual farming so he sharecropped his land. But he wasn't too old to make useful bamboo utensils. This was what he used to do during the winter months when his land sat fallow. But now, he had an annual contract to provide a steady quota of bamboo utensils to a wholesale distributor. It was good steady income for him, but more importantly, it kept him busy.

I used to sit and watch him weave. He would stand a five-foot section of bamboo on end, then split it down the middle. With his stubby sharp knife he'd cut one-sixteenth-of-an-inch thick strips down the length of the yellow fiber. Once he had a stack of these long strips, he'd sit down on his stool and begin weaving.

The thin bamboo strips would slide along his callused hands at high speed. His fingers moved so quickly that it was difficult to see exactly what he was doing to make the fibers take shape. In a matter of minutes, the base of a basket was done. Then he folded the loose ends upward and began weaving the side. He alternated the vertical bamboo with the horizontal ones, and again, in a matter of minutes, the small basket was all but finished. He took a pair of clippers and clipped the excess ends, then he wove a band across the top to hide the clipped ends. During this entire procedure, he would not speak. He produced a lot of baskets in one day.

There was a zen-like quality to his work. He had the ability to sit there, all day, everyday and weave baskets—he could clear his mind of all other thoughts but the routine of weaving one bamboo strip over or under another. It never seemed to bother him that he was doing the same movements over and over. What seemed important to him was that these repetitious movements were done correctly and precisely. His focus was so intense that I don't recall seeing him make a mistake. What fascinated me and what kept me watching him work was the anticipation of his making a mistake. But he never made one. He was a perfect human machine. In his mind, it would have been an embarrassment for him had he made a mistake. And in my presence, a mistake would have meant more than an embarrassment, but a loss of face.

The way he worked reminded me of Mr. Wu and his crew. They all had the same ability to make an infinite number of repetitive moves without letup or mental fatigue.

Interestingly, not once did grandpa Huang try to teach me how to weave the bamboo. He knew that he was teaching me by keeping me captivated with what he was doing. I suspect that had I stayed there long enough, I would have learned how simply by watching him work. At the very least, I remember enough of his work to describe it. So I did learn something, probably more than I realized.

Mom enrolled me at the nearby kindergarten to give both of us something productive to do while we were waiting for Governor Li to contact us. She volunteered to help with the children. And it wasn't long before Governor Li summoned her for an interview.

Mom's appointment with the governor took almost all day. The interview itself took only twenty minutes. Uncle Jin had already presented her credentials to the Governor. The meeting itself was a mere formality. She did, however, spend most of the day going to and from the Governor's secret headquarters.

She had left on a sampan in the morning, and was expected to return by late afternoon.

After school that day, I went directly to the public landing to wait for her. When I got there, I saw three men at the landing. They were intently watching the fourth man lead a steer down the riverbank onto the clean, wet cobblestones.

Two of the older children in my group knew what was about to happen. They looked on in awestruck silence. The younger children huddled behind them for protection. Something important was about to happen.

The man leading the steer swung his right leg up and climbed onto the animal's back. The steer flicked its tail and its flank twitched.

The man riding the steer slid a short, thick metal spike out of his tool pouch. He held it reverently in the palm of his left hand. Then he reached behind his back and withdrew a large heavy hammer from his belt. Carefully, almost gently he put the spike squarely in the center of the steer's skull. The hammer swung through the air and smacked against the iron spike. A hollow "thonk" shattered the silence. The steer's legs folded and the man jumped off its back as the stunned beast rolled onto its side. A second man rushed over to the fallen animal with a bucket and a knife. With one well placed cut, he severed the steer's neck artery.

The men used their buckets to collect the blood.

The butchers went about their work as if they were celebrating a harvest. They knew that for the next week or so, the entire village would feast on beef. But more than that, they would make a nice profit from selling the meat.

When Mom arrived at the landing, the butchers had the cut meat stacked neatly on large rectangular bamboo carrying trays. Even the bones of the large animal had been saved.

She saw me sitting on the edge of the cobblestone square, smiling and waving excitedly at her. She stepped gingerly ashore, trying to avoid the blood on the stone steps. She waved as she took in the sight.

Unable to contain my excitement, I told her what I had just seen.

I learned how to clean, skin and butcher a deer because of what I saw that day.

⌒➔

There were about thirty children ranging from kindergarten and younger to the sixth grade at the school. A teacher and her assistant ran the one room schoolhouse. The best thing about the facility was its playground. There were the usual swings and see-saws, but what made the place unusual was that a roof covered it. This was a building without any walls, just huge posts that supported the roof. During the rainy season, there was a place for the kids to play. This covered space also served as the town's meeting place and parade ground. Touring operas, acrobats, magicians, strongman and other attractions held performances here.

One day, there was a commotion by the parade ground. A big black Buick drove onto the grounds. Instantly, the teacher had the students stand, and in drill-sergeant fashion, marched the class out of the room.

Governor-General Li, dressed in his green-tinted khaki uniform, had appeared to inspect the school. The teachers bowed respectfully a number of times, obviously honored and delighted by the Governor's visit. The head teacher introduced the governor to the assembled children. "Good-morning, governor," the children chimed in unison.

The smiling general walked down the line of children and inspected us. He complimented the teacher on a job well done, whispered something to her then turned and walked to his car.

The teacher marched the kids to the covered playground then dismissed the class. But she took me aside and told me to go to the general's car. I had never been up close to a Buick before, so I ran to get a closer look. I stopped when the uniformed chauffeur opened the back door. Sitting in the back seat were Madame Li and her two young daughters. The girls were about my age.

Mrs. Li smiled and said: "It's all right. Don't be afraid. Come closer so that I can get a good look at you."

I obeyed when I saw the smile on Mom's face.

"How old are you?"

"Six."

"How would you like to go to school with my daughters?"

I looked at Mom, saw the hint of a nod so I said: "Ho ah," which is the Cantonese equivalent of OK.

"You think you'll get along with them?" Mrs. Li asked as her hand swept majestically in the direction of her girls.

I nodded.

"Good," she said. "Go on now. Go play," she commanded.

I walked away; glancing backwards, more interested in the car than seeing the two mothers talking.

A few minutes later, the big black Buick roared away.

Mom had just been officially hired to work for the governor.

(A car in China was a big deal in those days. Very few people had them, especially out here in the remote farming districts. What's more interesting was the fact that the name Buick stuck in my mind. It's probably as close to a Chinese word as any English word could be. Buick rolls off the Chinese tongue. Today, the Buick brand is as popular with the wealthy Chinese as it was then.)

A few days later, we left Grandfather Huang's house. It wasn't difficult to say goodbye. We were four people in one family divided by a regional dialect and a socio-economic chasm. Multiply this dysfunction across a country of 540 million people and you get an idea of the barrier to progress that faced China throughout her history.

About a year later, Grandpa Huang died. The governor was good enough to have his driver take us in the Buick to the funeral. Grandpa was buried on top of a hill overlooking the ruins of an ancient temple. His coffin was lowered into his own farmland so that he could be with his property forever. And he faced the temple ruins so that he could join the ancients in worship.

Grandma Huang moved in with her eldest son, a colonel in the Chinese Army. Colonel Huang was under the command of Governor-General Li. My uncle was ten years older than my father, but he didn't do as well in school. Much of the family savings went to my father's education, especially his sojourn at Yenching University and then Michigan. Had Dad returned to China with a PhD in philosophy from an American university, then he would have garnered enough prestige to be appointed to a high-level position in the Chinese bureaucracy. Assuming that he would pass some more civil service exams, of course.

Education and knowledge were the most valued assets that a person could acquire in life. These assets would move the family out of the country farm and into the world of the ruling elite. That was the Confucian dream: Let the smartest people rule the land.

Governor Li was a small frail-looking man. He looked years older than forty-seven. He was balding, which was unusual for a Chinese his age. His green-tinted khaki uniform always looked just a bit big on him. The material did not sit well on his small-boned frame. But he seemed to be a nice, affable man. The first time we met, he took me aside for a brief chat. I think he felt obligated to get to know his private secretary/translator's son.

"You have to speak up," he said, "I am nearly deaf in one ear, so I can't hear. An artillery shell landed near me and burst my eardrum. I was in the front lines with my troops," he told me. He probably said more, but this is what I remembered. Impressed, I told Mom about it.

"He is very proud of being on the front lines. He told me the same story," she said.

Madame Li was just a few inches shorter than her husband and quite a bit younger. She was thirty-two, only two years older than my mother. Today, we would probably call her a trophy wife. She always wore expensive, well-tailored silk cheongsams with slits that reached three-quarters of the way up her thighs. She had one daughter who was eight and another who was six, both of whom I had met when they visited my school. She knew that Mom had been educated in America and that her maiden name was Sun. She also believed that Mom was a relative of Dr. Sun Yat-sen, the George Washington of China, because they both have the same surname. Naturally, this bit of information gave Madame Li "Face." Clearly, she was in a position to hire an important person which further elevated her status. So, she perpetuated and even encouraged this little bit of talk in her social gatherings.

Rumor also began to circulate that my mother had attended the same American university as Madame

Chiang Kai-shek. Michigan is far from Wellesley, but no matter, Mom said.

Mom actually delighted in sharing Madame Li's foibles with me. At the time, it seemed quaint and harmless.

In time, both myths became accepted truths in her circle of friends. Madame Li couldn't have felt prouder as the employer of a member of the Sun family.

Mom found this situation disturbing and hypocritical, but she didn't say anything. She told me that this situation benefited us, though we didn't deserve it. The soldiers in the army revered Dr. Sun and we got special treatment because of Madame Li's belief. And Mom was not one to contradict her. As it turned out, this situation would benefit us as the war wore on.

More importantly, Madame Li wanted her children to learn English. It was her ambition for them to study in America. And if she could have her way, she would go to America, too. She thought that by getting on Mom's good side it would somehow help her achieve those goals.

Chapter Four
Gold

In 1938, Generalissimo Chiang Kai-shek, the man who ruled China, had appointed General Li Hanhun to protect the gold bullion stacked in the vaults of the Bank of Canton. To do this, Chiang also gave Li the additional title of Governor of Canton (Guangdong) Province as well as the Chairmanship of the Nationalist Party in the province. These promotions meant more power and better pay. As a General, Li commanded the 35th Army Group that defended Canton. As the governor, he was in charge of all the civil servants. The governor set policy, collected taxes, issued permits of all kinds, enforced the law and performed all the necessary duties to operate the business of the province. In short, Li had been given absolute control over the province—an area that bordered such important international cities as Hong Kong and Macao, not to mention one of China's oldest commercial cities, Canton itself. (Now Guangzhou.) Most of the foreign trade to southern China was funneled through this ancient port.

When Great Britain defeated China in the Opium Wars (1856-1860), she acquired Hong Kong for the very same reasons that Japan wanted Canton. Only Japan was more ambitious. She wanted all of China.

Strategically, Japan's long-range plan was to control the major ports in China. If she controlled the ports, then she would control trade, and control China, too. So, Japan attacked Canton just months after taking Shanghai. Shortly thereafter, the rest of the Chinese ports fell. What made the situation worse was that Generalissimo Chiang Kai-shek's armies could do nothing to stop the Japanese invasion. The only thing left for the Generalissimo to do was to save the gold locked in the vaults of the Bank of Canton. And that's what Governor-General Li did. The general moved the gold to his new provincial headquarters in Shaoguan.

When we got to Shaoguan in 1942, our assigned living quarters was a store on a narrow cobblestone street. In fact, all the stores on this long block of one-story row houses had been emptied. The former residents had been relocated. They had been evicted to make room for the arrival of the government's employees.

These gray brick houses with gray tiled roofs were roughly sixteen-by-forty feet with hard dirt floors and a high-pitched ceiling. It was one big open, empty room. Two small windows hung on the back wall, but they didn't have glass in them. Instead, white, lacquered paper covered the openings. Six tall movable panels made up the front of the shops. The entire front of the building could be opened to the street. Merchandise could be displayed in the front portion while the owner's family lived in the back.

The army had furnished the one room with two army cots, a small field table and a bamboo-folding chair. The sparse furnishings sat in the middle of this large cavernous room. The setting only served to emphasize the desolation and emptiness of war-torn China.

Officers on the general's staff and civilian bureaucrats occupied the other houses on the street. The provincial bureaucrats were particularly noticeable because they didn't wear khaki uniforms. They wore Mandarin robes, usually black or dark blue. Wherever Governor Li established his headquarters, that place would also be the temporary capitol of Canton Province.

The governor's family and servants occupied a large house with a circular pond in front, not far from where we were. I used to fish there in the summer.

As the war wore on, the center of power began to unravel. Lacking food, money and a cohesive plan to manage the operations of the area under Li's command, local politicians, minor warlords, and civic leaders bombarded the governor with requests for aid.

Each wanted their share of the province's tax money. Mom spent much of her time dealing with these requests. Most of the letters pleaded for money and food while many addressed grievances concerning corruption and the unconscionable behavior among the upper ranks of the bureaucracy. Mandarins and bureaucrats demanded outright bribes to get permits and other necessary official documentation. No bribe, no permit.

People with cash could buy government approval for anything they wanted. It appeared that the Governor-General was neither acting as a bona fide governor nor was he conducting himself like a true military commander. General Li was content with the status quo. As long as the Japanese made no moves, he was content. He could continue to collect taxes and run the province as he wished.

Mom could do nothing with the requests for food or money. The government storehouses were down to emergency reserves, she had been told. And paper money held little real value. Those with tangible and real assets to sell could not see their way clear to exchange their goods for pieces of printed paper. Especially when that paper is backed by a corrupt and possibly bankrupt government. But this was just part of the currency problem. Since Japan controlled trade in the coastal cities, any goods purchased in

Japanese-occupied territory had to be paid for with occupation money. Once these goods reached free China for sale, they were bought with Chinese money.

Neither side would officially accept the other side's currency. Black market money changers exploited the situation and played one currency against the other. The value of the Japanese currency would increase with each victory, while the Chinese currency would decrease in value as the country fell into further disarray.

This situation gave the currency traders a field day. No matter what happened, they made money. The situation was so complex that few government officials had the ability or inclination to deal with it. So they let the situation fester.

Regular people, however, were reluctant to accept paper money for goods and services. They wanted gold and silver. Short of that, bartering became a popular form of exchange. At least you knew what you were getting. You could exchange an apple for an orange, which was a lot simpler than understanding the valuations of the two combatant's currencies.

Mom would brief the governor on the letters that complained of corruption, theft and bribery. She thought that he ought to know, but the governor merely shrugged his shoulders. "What can I do," he asked rhetorically. "These matters are best left to the magistrates and the Mandarins. My concern is the Japanese."

This all too frequent response finally got to Mom. Why didn't the magistrates and Mandarins do anything about this situation? To find out, she reached out to discover the scope and magnitude of the problem.

What she discovered was much worse than what she had first thought. All the written complaints were mild compared to the one-on-one grievances that she heard. It took courage for these men and women to speak their minds. Clearly, these people were willing to voice their concerns because they feared famine and economic collapse. More important, people were speaking out because they sensed that it was now safe to do it. The complainants included local dignitaries who were already thinking about their positions in life after the war; wealthy families who had been watching their fortunes being taxed away by unscrupulous tax collectors; and the intelligentsia who naturally abhor corruption in government in any form, not to mention the revulsion of the idealistic young. They were all testing the waters.

Unfortunately, the chain of corruption led directly to the governor's cronies. Which was why the magistrates and the Mandarins did nothing.

To make things more complicated, some people in unoccupied China began to value the Japanese currency more than the Chinese Yuan. They hedged their paper-money positions because the Chinese Armies could not stop the Japanese. (In November, 1944, for example, the people of Kweilin (Quilin) lost everything to the conquering Japanese. Whatever Chinese money they had was suddenly worthless. Kweilin is only about 250 miles from Canton, as the crow files.)

But what bothered people the most was the unequal and unfair taxation. High-ranking government officials arbitrarily imposed taxes wherever and on whomever they thought they could extort money. And these tax dollars did not go to servicing the general good, but disappeared into private pockets.

Responsible, civic-minded people desperately implored their Governor-General to end the corruption, re-establish order and strengthen the currency. They wanted a return to the good old days.

During those good old days, Mandarins achieved their rank and position through the Confucian Examination System, which was created about 2,500 years ago. Theoretically, if you scored perfectly in all of your exams, i.e. from local, to district, to provincial and, finally, to the national level, then you could end up being the prime minister. That's assuming that you scored well as you moved up in the level of difficulty. The most difficult exam was at the national level.

Conversely, a low score, at any level, would keep you where you were in the bureaucratic hierarchy with little chance of advancement. Thus, there was a risk to taking the next level of the exam. You could lose face by not scoring well. Everybody would think that you're a dummy. So the tendency was to find your level and stay there.

This civil-service exam system clearly rewarded the best and brightest. They would get the highest ranks in the government. In theory, according to Confucius, the smartest people in the land would administer and govern the country. Furthermore, they would get an 'iron rice bowl.' Once you got a perfect or near perfect score in an exam, nobody can take that achievement away from you. And once you receive your appointment as a high-ranking Mandarin, you would be paid no matter what because civil servants administered and controlled the country's finances, hence the iron rice bowl. You would always eat.

During the stable, strong, prosperous Dynastic periods, this system worked well. But, by 1938, China was broke. The Japanese invasion made matters worse. It was difficult for a tax collector because people didn't have the money. Nevertheless, taxes had to be collected, no matter what the circumstances, otherwise the government couldn't function.

For the government to function, lower tax dollars meant lower wages for the civil servants. Everybody had to take a cut. This situation was conducive to abuse. And the seeds for this abuse had been sowed ages ago.

One of the ancient Chinese traditions was that if someone did you a favor, you returned the favor by giving that person a gift. The size or value of this gift depended on the value of the favor bestowed. The bigger the favor, the bigger the gift.

Grandpa Sun once employed a man to drive the family's rickshaw. It was clear to grandpa that this man did not have the aptitude to learn how to drive a car. To help his employee adapt to a new technological environment, i.e., the coming automobile, grandpa encouraged this man to save his money and perhaps buy a farm. Grandpa then helped him invest his savings in a railroad. The stock in the rail company did very well, so much so that the man could buy a farm with his savings. The farm prospered, and every year since, this man would deliver a wagon load of watermelons to grandpa's house every summer. Grandpa never asked for this annual gift. It was an ancient social custom that was practiced by all, no matter your social status. The man literally shared the fruits of his labor with grandpa out of gratitude for helping him change his life.

This Confucian ideal of education and civility has permeated the Chinese unconscious to such an extent that it is ingrained into the way we behave and interact with each other.

In Canton Province during the war, high-ranking Mandarins who had been used to a prosperous lifestyle naturally wanted to continue living that way. And since the gift-giving tradition was voluntary, a general decline in the economy meant a corresponding decline in gifts. To maintain their standard of living, some high-ranking bureaucrats began to supplement their incomes by subtly asking for a gift. This was in violation of the Confucian tradition. It was not socially acceptable to do that. And if the subtlety didn't register, they would go beyond social mores and ask for an outright bribe if you wanted something from the government. And as everyone knows, a government official can make life miserable for you if you got on his wrong side, particularly in the case of a tax collector.

The lower-level bureaucrats saw what their leaders were doing, so they began to behave in the same way. The culture of corruption began to take hold at every level of government.

This situation was totally intolerable in several ways. It was a corruption of the Confucian ideal, and it promoted distrust between those who governed and those who are governed. Mom felt that something had to be done. But what?

⌒

From 1938 to 1944, Japan occupied a hundred-mile semi-circular ring of territory that included Hong Kong and Canton. This was their stronghold in the Pearl River Delta area. Then, in April, 1944, the Japanese made a major push inland. Their Twenty-Third Army left Canton and marched west toward Liuchow airfield. This army completely bypassed Shaoguan, which was due north of Canton.

About five hundred miles north of Shaoguan, the Eleventh Japanese Army headed south from Wuchang to take Changsha, a march of about two hundred miles.

These two Japanese Armies would meet in the middle, crushing any Chinese resistance in their way. Their objectives were six US/Chinese Airfields along a five-hundred-mile corridor that stretched across four provinces.

On June 18, 1944 the city of Changsha fell.

On August 8, the airfield at Hengyang was taken.
September 4, Lingling Airfield.
November 10, Kweilin.
November 11, Liuchow.
November 24, Nanning.

The attacks were so well coordinated that the Japanese Northern Army reached Kweilin on November 10; while the Southern Army from Canton reached Liuchow on November 11. These two airfields are separated by a mere 100 miles. Both Japanese Armies had covered over three hundred miles on their march across central China.

Ultimately, the Japanese advanced beyond Kweilin. Their armies were only 300 miles from Chungking, the war-time capital of China. Japan was well on her way to conquering all of China by the end of 1944.

General Li's 35th Army Group could not stop the Japanese. In fact, the Japanese had completely by-passed General Li's position at Shaoguan. He saw no action during this Japanese advance. His strategy was to retreat and keep his army out of harm's way.

Then, finally on February 1945, the Japanese took Suichuan airfield, which was roughly one hundred miles north of where Governor-General Li's 35th Army Group was. Suichuan airfield is located at the strategic juncture of three provinces: Canton, Kiangsi and Fukien.

The arrows show the coordinated Japanese troop movements in taking the US/Chinese Air Bases during April 1944 to April 1945.

The Chinese high command was in a state of shock, if not panic because Japan had, effectively, conquered China. Mom knew that Generalissimo Chiang Kai-shek's armies could do nothing to stop the Japanese. As for General Li's army, the best that his staff could do was to huddle over the map plotting the best escape route and debating the wisdom of a surrender.

Interestingly, Japan made this bold audacious move in China at a time when it was losing the war everywhere else. American B-29 bombers had been hitting both the Japanese supply lines and the main islands of Japan from these Chinese airfields. While the Japanese captured them, this did not stop the B-29's. The Americans moved some of their planes inland and others to the new airfields in the Mariana Islands. The bombings continued from these new locations.

Japan was losing the war in the Pacific, but they knew that they could win the ground war in China. Their adversary was weak because of the corruption and a poor fighting spirit. Using 700,000 soldiers, the largest Japanese troop action during the war, their armies cut through the heart of China from Kaifeng in the north, all the way to Vietnam. In a little over seven months, they had captured a one-thousand-mile-long corridor down the middle of China. (As a comparison, only 22,000 Japanese soldiers fought and died on Iwo Jima.)

Their strategy was to stop the bombings from Chinese airfields and at the same time capture the mainland. They could always use China as a bargaining chip with the allies. Japanese intelligence knew that the American military was anticipating mind-boggling casualties if the Allied forces were to land on the beaches of the main Japanese island. The Americans were not looking forward to losing one million men against the suicidal Japanese.

On the other side, the Japanese high command was still thinking in the old-fashioned way of a nego-tiated peace. They would use China as a bargaining chip to secure an armistice with the allies. This strategy would save a million American lives on the beaches of Japan.

China and a million American lives in exchange for peace with Japan.

In January of 1945, during this Japanese offen-sive, the temperatures at Governor Li's Provincial Headquarters hovered in the 40s and rose to a pleas-ant 60 or higher by noon. Not far from his house was his big black Buick parked with rows of trucks that formed the motor pool. Next to these vehicles were tall stacks of metal gasoline drums. Hundreds of fifty-five gallon drums of precious gasoline filled the large fenced-in compound.

The men in the motor pool generally looked after me. I liked to watch the mechanics work on those big army trucks. I didn't have to go to school simply because there wasn't one. And I didn't like being tutored along with the general's children. They made me feel like a second-class citizen, an employee's child. When I described the situation and my unhappiness at being treated like a servant, Mom agreed to let me "work" with the soldiers instead. Clearly, there are different ways to learn about life.

An old man guarded the compound that stored the gasoline supply for the army. He was thin and frail as if he had not been properly fed for most of his life. He sat by the big wooden doors guarding the tall stacks of precious flammable liquid. The heavy odor of gas permeated the area, but he had gotten used to the smell. On cold mornings, he would crack the big door a foot or two to let the sun warm him. But the sun didn't provide enough heat to suit him. Between his feet and in front of his rocking chair sat a chipped and dented white-enamel wash basin. The basin had a rounded bottom and it was about twelve inches in diameter and four inches deep. In the middle of this metal basin were lumps of hot, glowing coals.

He sunned himself, smoked his pipe and warmed his feet and hands over his portable stove. He seemed oblivious to the gasoline stacked behind him.

Seeing a ready and available audience, he would call me over to join him. "Sit and warm yourself," he said.

I used to sit on my haunches in front of the glowing red charcoal and listen to his stories.

"My boy," the old man said, "do you know how many years I've been working for the general? Thirty. Thirty years," he said proudly. "I was his rickshaw driver. When he got a car, he got rid of the rickshaw. But he still thinks very highly of me. And do you know why? Because I'm important to him. He trusts me. I'm not like the others who deal in the black market," he said with pride.

He raised his right arm and pointed his thumb at the drums just behind his shoulder. "You know how much money they charge for gasoline? I could make a fortune, I tell you. But the general trusts me. That's why he put me here, to watch over his gasoline. This is a very important job, watching the gasoline. There are thieves everywhere. That's why the gasoline is here, behind this compound where no one can steal it. Smart huh? Yeah, the general is very smart. He's smart to keep me here to watch over things for him."

I sat and listened, but it wasn't long before the old man ran out of stories. When he began to repeat himself, I lost interest. I drifted away to watch the mechanics work on the trucks.

Then, one cold morning, there was a loud commotion at the gas depot. Thick, black, heavy smoke bellowed into the sky, followed by a loud roar and a huge ball of fire. In seconds, the entire area was consumed by thick pitch-black smoke. A huge black cloud mushroomed high into the sky. The metal drums of gasoline had completely disappeared. The heat from the flames peeled the paint off the nearby trucks. Hundreds of soldiers ran about tossing buckets of water on anything that was in flames.

Half dazed and blackened by smoke, the old man staggered about in the center of a circle of angry soldiers. "It wasn't my fault," he cried, "I fell asleep, that's all." Then he turned wildly to grab a nearby soldier. "It wasn't my fault!" the old man screamed for everyone to hear. "The pan tipped over." When he realized what he had just said, he covered his face and fell to his knees.

A soldier cursed him then roughly pushed him to the ground.

Mom ran into the circle of soldiers. "Has anyone seen my son?" she cried several times.

Luckily, I was in the truck repair area, away from the gasoline. I waved and called out to her.

"Thank goodness you are all right!"

The old man sobbed. "Someone turned over my pan...they...they...I couldn't stop the fire. It just got bigger and bigger..." The ring of angry soldiers glared unmercifully at him. The Old Man propped himself up on one elbow. His body trembled uncontrollably with fear and panic.

Mom grabbed my hand and forcefully took me away. She knew what was about to happen.

Then I heard two shots.

Everything was in complete shambles. The decision had already been made. We would have to evacuate immediately. The general was certain that the huge column of black smoke could be readily seen by the Japanese. The threat of the oncoming Japanese was foremost on everyone's mind.

Mom took me aside to explain the situation.

"You know, the fire is a very bad thing. The Japanese will see the black smoke. They are very close. We have to leave now," she said firmly. Behind her, high up in the air, a long column of black smoke lingered in the cold blue sky.

"Where are we going?"

"We are going inland, away from the Japanese. The entire army is leaving."

"Are we going in the Buick?"

"The car is only big enough for the general's family. His children and their amahs will leave first. We will follow later with the rest of the army." Then she sat down beside me and took my hand. "I'm going in one of the trucks with all the important papers." She paused to clear her throat. "You'll be going with the soldiers. The sergeant of the motor pool will be in charge of you. You do what he tells you," she said. "We won't be separated for long. Five days at most."

I was nine at the time. That would make it four years since Mom and I escaped from Shanghai. And during those four years, whatever fears that I might have had, had been locked up inside of me. I hadn't sobbed or cried when the Japanese soldier patted me on the top of my head. My hand didn't tremble when I gave him his roll of money. In fact, I remember calmly looking up at him, as if this were the most important game in the world. And it was because I had fooled him.

During those four, formative years, fear was not an emotion that I exhibited. It wasn't a question of male pride that to show fear would mean being weak. I was too young to know about the macho aspect of being a "man." After all, I was a young boy whose hormones hadn't developed sufficiently to experience that macho feeling. I focused on being a good, obedient boy because that's what boys are supposed to do.

When Mom told me that we might be separated for five days, I knew what she had really meant to say. There had always been the possibility that we would not survive. This had always been the unspoken truth. This time was no different, though the circumstances might have been more intense and threatening.

Under these circumstances, I nearly always thought that the worst thing that could happen to me was to die. Once that thought crossed my mind, fear was not the issue. Survival was.

In fact, I told her that I hope she had enough gasoline in her truck to make the trip. Then we would meet at the end of it. That was our only choice.

$$\sim$$

To re-supply Li's army with gas, American transport planes would have to fly the precious liquid from

Burma over the Himalayas into Kunming. From there, the gas would be trucked over hundreds of miles of twisting, narrow dirt roads. But even that was no longer possible. The Japanese blitzkrieg had taken a corridor of land from Vietnam in the south all the way up to Peking (Beijing) and into Manchuria. Their 1944 offensive had cut China in half. The Japanese owned the middle section of China, leaving the western portion of the country to the Generalissimo, and a portion of the coast between Shanghai and Canton to Governor-General Li.

General Li was now completely isolated from the wartime capital of Chungking. His territory consisted of a bulge of land that included the eastern portion of Canton Province; Fukien Province to the East; and most of Kiangsi Province to the North. The General was left on his own. There was no contact between him and his commander, Generalissimo Chiang Kai-shek.

During the entire war, Governor-General Li had not faced the Japanese in a major battle. This time, he retreated from Shaoguan to Longchuan.

Longchuan is about 170 miles to the southeast on the banks of the East (Dong) River.

The arrow shows Governor-General Li's retreat from Shaoguan to Longchuan into unoccupied territory.

Suddenly, the gold from the Bank of Canton was in danger once more. With the gasoline supply gone, the soldiers siphoned the fuel out of most of the trucks and topped off as many as they could. The vehicles with empty fuel tanks were abandoned.

The gold, along with the important files, was loaded onto the operational vehicles.

135

Mom traveled by truck with the rest of the high-ranking bureaucrats and army officers. Many sat on the crates of bullion. She was going ahead to help set up a new office and find a place for us to live.

Thousands of foot soldiers earned their names. They walked.

The sergeant ordered me into an open bamboo sedan chair mounted between two thick bamboo-carrying poles. Two soldiers, one at each end, hoisted the poles onto their shoulders. I had an unobstructed view of the road as I bounced along in rhythm with the soldier's steps, my head a foot or so above theirs. I could see two long lines of foot soldiers winding down the single-lane dirt road. Each line hugged the ditch on either side. The men were prepared to dive for cover the moment they heard an aircraft engine.

At the first sound of an aircraft engine, my two soldiers would lift the bamboo poles off their shoulders, take a few quick steps into the ditch and drop me to the ground. The three of us would huddle together for protection. Luckily, the bullets whizzed by missing us. I have no idea how close we were to death because my two army buddies were on top of me and my face was buried in the dirt.

But not everyone was so lucky. The loses were heavy because we were in flat farmland with very little cover. The wounded suffered unbearable pain because we had no morphine. Many wounds were wrapped with the uniforms of the dead. We had no medics. Men died unnecessarily for the lack of sanitary bandages and professional care.

Once, we thought we heard an aircraft engine and promptly dove for the ditch. It turned out to be a truck. When the vehicle roared by, nearly all the soldiers waved an obscene gesture at that unlucky driver.

Luckily for me, I had been protected by my two buddies. (I'm sad to say that I don't remember their names. In hindsight, they probably saved my life during our march together.) While I saw the wounded and heard the dying moans and cries, they insulated themselves and me from the trauma. We lowered our gaze and adopted a detached feeling of resignation. We huddled beside a stone roadside shrine for protection. There weren't many ways to insulate yourself against such inhumane conditions.

After all, the worst thing that could happen to us is that we would die. Fortunately, it didn't come to that. After that first day, the Japanese left us alone, probably because they were running short of bullets, too. Besides, they had already won. There wasn't much we could do to fight back.

The march from Shaoguan to Longchuan, our ultimate destination, took much longer than anyone had expected. We weren't sure where we were going since the battlefield was fluid and the intelligence faulty. The Japanese was moving toward Suichuan Airfield, which was just northeast of our location. So we headed southeast to avoid them. Good thing we did because they took that airfield in February, just weeks after the fire.

Mom had nearly given up on ever seeing me again. We were walking which took much longer than her ride in the truck. And the army had taken the long way around to avoid running into the Japanese. Meanwhile she waited and waited, getting more anxious with each passing day. It didn't help that there was no news. The Chinese Army didn't have any working radios. Finally, two weeks later, I caught up with her. Our reunion was subdued. Though we were joyous to be reunited, our happiness had been overshadowed by the constant pang of hunger. Our rations had been cut to the bone. We hadn't had any meat in weeks.

Perhaps the happiest man there was Sergeant Wong, the man in the motor pool who had been ordered to look after me. He was happy and relieved to have delivered me, unharmed, to my mother. As a reward, she shared her last can of Spam with him and my two buddies who had carried me across the mountains. Mom had been saving the meat for a special occasion, and this was it. But we had to eat it in secret, away from everyone. This can of Spam was probably the last one in China.

For the Japanese to win, all they had to do was just sit and watch us starve to death.

Most days, we had little to eat that winter. What kept us alive was watery, meatless congee that the soldiers cooked. I'm not sure why the motor-pool soldiers took me to be one of their own, but they did. Maybe it was because of the rumor that Mom and I were related to Dr. Sun Yat-sen, but I'll never know.

What I do know is that we spent most our days scrounging for food. By the time we settled into our new location, the spring planting season still hadn't arrived yet. Crops don't grow overnight. Or in the cold. The army's food reserves were dangerously low because we didn't have the trucks to take the army's food supply with us. We could only take what we could carry or load onto pushcarts. The whole thing was a disaster.

The government used to print truckloads of money to pay, house, feed and equip the soldiers. But now that we've been cut off and isolated by the Japanese, even the soldiers' pay couldn't be delivered.

Many soldiers deserted. If they weren't going to be paid or fed properly, then they might as well go home to be with their families. The prospects might be better there. But they weren't the only people to leave.

My two buddies and I were sitting in the middle of a rice field looking forlornly at the fallow land wishing that there were rice to be harvested. And as we sat there contemplating the land, I heard yelling and screaming from the nearby farmhouse. A family of four was being driven out of their home.

Puzzled, I turned and asked what was going on?

"The army has requisitioned their farm," came the sad reply. "These peasants have been ordered to leave." Two soldiers with rifles and bayonets goaded the peasants off their land.

"Why?"

My buddies were unsure of how to answer the question. "Maybe you should ask your mother," came the reply.

I ran home. Mom confirmed the fact that General Li had ordered the removal of the peasants from their homes so that the army would have enough food for the troops. It was a tragic and heartrending sight, to see families with children forcefully removed from their homes. More tragic still because whatever food reserves that they had was confiscated, too. The peasants were only allowed to take what they could carry.

Many of the soldiers couldn't look these people in the eyes because they knew that they would be eating the farmers' winter rice reserves.

Henceforth, the army would take over the farms and work the fields. The general wanted to control the food supply. The only way he could keep his authority was to own a standing army. And the only way to keep his army was to feed it.

Since the majority of the general's recruits had been peasants themselves, they knew that the shortage of food would get much worse before it got better. Furthermore, they sympathized with the men, women and children who had been driven out of their ancestral farms.

Disillusioned and angry soldiers abandoned their positions and disappeared into the countryside. They took the only things of value with them: their rifles and bullets. But that practice was quickly stopped when their weapons were stored under lock and key.

Former officers turned themselves into warlords, promising their followers a better life and a better government. These newly minted warlords carved out their own territories. Many had received financial backing from friends and family. Their strategy was to negotiate a permanent position with Chiang

Kai-shek after the war. China was reverting to the days of fiefdoms and overlords. These people no longer had any faith or trust in the central government.

Mean spirited people turned themselves into bands of roaming bandits. Those with rifles and bullets became leaders of these gangs. One gang terrorized the Yangtze River. They would swoop down the side of the mountain to capture passenger junks and hold these people for ransom. Worse, they would sell captured young girls to anyone who had the money to buy one. More disheartening was the fact that there were people who bought these girls.

There was no one to stop these criminals. Chaos ruled because no one else could.

And what happened to the displaced peasants? Many died from starvation. Those who survived had nowhere to go but straight into the arms of Mao Tse-tung and the Communists. They joined Mao's peasant army because he promised to share their hunger with them and not take food from the mouths of their children. Mao promised that they would fight and work together to get what was rightfully theirs. And everyone would share in the bounty, not just the privileged few.

Mom tried hard to maintain an optimistic attitude for my benefit, but it didn't work. Both of us worried about food and where our next meal would come from. I didn't know any better, but Mom worried about our health and our daily intake of protein. We were always hunting for farms that had egg-laying chickens. I don't remember the details of how it happened or why, but at one point, the only thing that Mom and I had to eat that day was one hard-boiled egg. And we paid dearly for that egg, too. After all, you can't eat gold.

I'm ashamed to say that we probably survived that winter because the army rationed the peasants' rice reserves for our use. And I can't help but wonder whether we all could have survived had we shared and rationed the rice rather than forcefully throwing the peasants off their land. Maybe this thought is too humanitarian and liberal to contemplate.

⟳

Chapter Five
The Theft

But the general's gold was another story. This most important commodity from the Bank of Canton had been loaded onto the trucks first. In the chaos and panic of the aftermath of the gasoline fire, boxes of sensitive and top-secret files had been thrown, almost willy-nilly, into the trucks, too.

In her hunt for some of her papers, Mom had stumbled on a few files that had not been intended to be seen by anyone. At least Mom had not seen these files before. These were the ledger books and inventory sheets for the gold from the Bank of Canton. More importantly, what really got her attention was a folder full of receipts from a Swiss bank. There were no names on the Swiss documents. Just numbers. There were two numbered accounts.

Guiltily and with a slight tremble in her hands, she covered the box. She knew she had stumbled onto something that she shouldn't have seen. Quickly she put the box in the back of the truck, exactly where she had found it. What frightened her was that there were two numbered accounts. There was only one conclusion to be drawn from this, and that is that one of them belonged to Chiang Kai-shek and the other to Governor-General Li. Only the most powerful of men could move the gold from the middle of China all the way to Switzerland. Clearly, she had to keep this information to herself. She told herself to pretend that she never saw these files. If Li found out that she knew, then our lives could be in danger. On the other hand, this information, if used properly, could be the downfall of the corrupt regime.

My mother's discovery of the movement of the gold bullion into two numbered Swiss bank accounts explained a lot of things. For starters, she suddenly realized why the provincial civil servants, particularly the higher-ranking ones that were closest to the general, had been so bold in their efforts to collect bribes and to intimidate the average citizen.

To move heavy bricks of gold from the middle of China all the way to Swiss banks required the participation of a lot of people. The highest levels of government officials had to approve such a transfer otherwise the paperwork authorizing the movement of these assets across numerous international borders could not have been created. This high-level participation also ensured the safety of the eventual delivery of the bullion. No transport company or individual would risk his life to interfere with this transaction. The power behind this move had to be absolute, and everyone involved had to know it. Otherwise the gold could just vanish without the possibility of retribution. For these reasons, Mom concluded that Chiang Kai-shek had to be the owner of one of those numbered accounts.

The other aspect of this move was that many people, not just the high-level ones, had to be involved. Moving this heavy metal took manpower, from the original packers of the shipments, to the people who would load them onto the camels for the long trek across the old Silk Route. The general's closest cronies knew what was going on because the general did not put the bullion on the trucks by himself, nor did he pack them for shipment to Switzerland. Hence, these trusted cronies had something on their boss. They knew that their leader had committed a crime.

If it were permissible for people at the top to behave like this, then what would stop the lower-level ones from exercising their own brand of corruption within their own little fiefdoms? The answer was: nothing. They were all co-conspirators in a brazen act to enrich themselves at the expense of the general public.

For over a year, Mom had been trying to figure out why the provincial government was so corrupt. Now she knew. She secretively shared this latest information with May and Jin. Working together, they had contacted and personally spoken with powerful people across a wide spectrum of businesses and political affiliations. It was clear that this corrupt culture had not only weakened the province, but the nation as a whole. A nation cannot be strong if her leaders were only concerned with their individual well-being and not the welfare of the nation as a whole. The selfish attitude of the ruling elite corrupted the entire nation. China was both morally and economically bankrupt.

But the event that pulled all of the disapproving players together was the gasoline fire. The people that Mom had been talking with were now willing to act. It was time to finalize their plan to make some changes. For her own protection, Mom said nothing about the gold or the numbered accounts. Nor would May and Jin. The three of them were afraid for our lives.

In total secret, they set the meeting at a Mandarin's summer retreat. The ancient house was far from any neighbors. There were centuries-old shade trees mixed with exotic plants and flowers surrounding the modest single-story building. A peaceful rustic silence greeted us as we approached the historic house. Other revolutions and uprisings had been plotted here across a few Dynasties. Mom held my hand as she led the way up the crushed stone path. She always took me to these secret meetings. If at all possible, she didn't want us to be separated. She used me as an excuse to get away from the office; a doctor's appointment or some other family excuse. She wanted me around because she was about to meet with a roomful of powerful men. They were all high-ranking officials from the nearby provinces— mayors, magistrates, district commissioners and the like. She had reasoned that no self-respecting Mandarin would make any untoward advances on a married woman with a child in tow. More importantly, she didn't want to take a chance on losing me during these uncertain times. And, as it turned out, this would be the last and most memorable meeting of its kind.

As usual, I waited for her outside. I inspected all the cars and talked with the chauffeurs. A few of them let me look under the hoods of their limousines. Unfortunately, none of them would let me blow the horn. They would put their index finger to their lips to indicate quiet, then point at the house. And, to be egalitarian, I talked with the rickshaw drivers and sedan-chair carriers, too. They had nothing to do, and neither did I.

The hideaway housed a most unusual group of powerful local political leaders. Many of them belonged to Uncle Jin's underground network, though none of them knew that they were connected in this way. They included people from nearby Fukien and Kiangsi Provinces. These men, and they were all men with the exception of Mom, felt that this meeting had national significance, rather than merely Provincial ones. They felt no allegiance to the governor of another province. More important, they had been appalled by the fact that General Li blew up his own gasoline supply through sheer stupidity and negligence. This was just inexcusable. It was further proof to the western world that China was, indeed, a backward and ignorant nation. And this unpleasant thought galled them. This once proud ancient nation was tired of being a backward, third-world, fifth-rate country. The anguish and anger was palpable in that room.

These important people had gathered there with one purpose in mind: to determine the fate of Governor-General Li, and by implication, the nation. The thinking was that once news of the gasoline debacle reached the High Command in Chungking, Chiang Kai-shek would have to make some changes. And this group wanted a say in making those changes.

Perhaps more conducive to change was the fact that General Joseph Stilwell, the man that President

Roosevelt (FDR) had put in charge of the China-Burma-India Theatre had a very low opinion of Generalissimo Chiang Kai-shek. And Stilwell didn't hide his disdain. The general called Chiang Kai-shek, that "little peanut", not to the Generalissimo's face, of course, but only to his superior FDR, and his subordinates in Chungking. American disdain for the Generalissimo was universal among General Stilwell's staff. Only a delusional egomaniac would have the gall to call himself "The Generalissimo" of a poor, feeble country. A grand title isn't going to make China great and powerful.

In the eyes of the Chinese politicians, looking inept in front of the American high command reflected poorly on all of them. This was a classic case of a loss of Face. They felt ashamed of themselves and their country. Their national pride had been hurt by Li's ineptitude.

Additionally, they knew that the peasants, who had been thrown off their farms, had linked up with Mao Tse-tung's peasant army. The group's fear of Communism helped them overcome any remaining doubts. It was time for them to go against the status quo. China needed a change. And they felt that it would be better to change from the inside, rather than have change dictated by the Communists.

This group of patriotic people drafted a powerful document. The list of grievances and misdeeds was long and substantial. The top two items on this list were the mishandling of the gasoline reserves and, secondarily, a request for an audit of the assets in the Bank of Canton. Uncle Jin had suggested the audit since corruption ruled the province. The request for a financial audit was the prudent thing to do, especially under these chaotic circumstances. This rationale made common sense, but more importantly, it wiped away all suspicions of a hidden agenda for the accounting of the gold. This would be a general audit of all of the provincial assets.

The fact that the missing gold could not be accounted for would not only throw suspicion on the general, but also serve as an unspoken warning to Chiang Kai-shek. As a consummate politician, Chiang would want to distance himself from this political time bomb. Under the present dire economic circumstances, Chiang's enemies, particularly the Communists, would want to turn this disgraceful situation into political capital.

Additionally, bureaucratic misdeeds such as blatant requests for bribes, and in some cases outright extortion, were also cataloged. The document clearly spelled out the corruption that permeated the entire regime under the Governor-General Li's command. No names were actually attached to the misdeeds. This was done to ensure tranquility amongst the brethren of leaders. They knew that misfortune could happen to any of them. People still had lives to lead after the war. If nothing else, Confucius preached compassion. Politics should not be a blood sport. Everyone could be reeducated to follow the Confucian way.

The anonymous document was hand-delivered to an American liaison officer who passed it along to Generalissimo Chiang Kai-shek.

This American intelligence officer had no knowledge of who the authors of the letter were nor would he disclose from whom he had received it. Besides, he was not under the command of the Generalissimo and he had no obligation or duty to reveal any confidences that had been entrusted to him. Most important is the fact that a friendly envoy had delivered this damning document to Chiang Kai-shek and not to his political enemies.

Everyone involved hoped that this warning shot in the direction of the Generalissimo would produce results. Under the circumstances, they knew that Chiang would, at the very minimum, release Li from his duties. But the ultimate gesture would be a clean sweep of the entire provincial regime.

*Front row, left to right: Unknown Mandarin/bureaucrat, Madame Li,
unknown Mandarin/bureaucrat, Governor-General Li Hanhun.*

*Back row, left to right: Unknown civil servant, unknown officer, Jane
Sun Huang, American officer at a meeting sometime in the winter of
1944-1945.*

*My mother is the lone woman at this meeting
sometime in the winter of 1944-1945.*

The war ended in China on a hot, bright sunny August day. The one radio we had blared out the news. The Japanese had surrendered to China and Great Britain on August 15 in accordance with the terms of the Potsdam Declaration. We had electricity because this was the location of the provincial government. In the countryside, word of Japan's defeat flew across the land at the speed of sound. In some remote regions, the news came a bit slower because people had to carry the word to the next village. Eventually, everybody knew.

Then on September 1, 1945, one day before the Japanese signed the formal surrender aboard the battleship U.S.S. Missouri, Generalissimo Chiang Kai-shek, the supreme military-civilian ruler of China, asked Governor-General Li, the supreme military-civilian leader of Canton Province, to resign.

Li Hanhun, his family and servants were shipped off, down the East (Dong) River, back to their home in Canton.

Li's entire staff, cronies and thousands of corrupt civil servants were also let go. There was a complete shakeup in the provincial government.

With the Japanese surrender, their occupational currency suddenly became worthless. Those who lived in the occupied zones were holding colored paper. To avoid complete chaos, Chiang's government promised to exchange the Japanese money for the yuan. People were ordered to use the Japanese currency to conduct daily business until this exchange could be made. Most Chinese were living in a world of uncertainties, wondering what was going to happen next.

Meanwhile, Mom was asked to go to Chungking for a debriefing.

But the saga was far from over. Our paths with the Li's would cross again in Shanghai.

⌁

The way to Chungking was mostly one-lane dirt roads. The mode of transport was an army truck. And we were lucky to get it. Whatever resources the army had were being used to round up the Japanese. The overwhelming issue at hand was the building of prison compounds to house the POWs. The first thing was to put them all into prisons, mostly for their own protection. Feeding the Japanese was a secondary problem. No one had any sympathy for a starving Japanese soldier on Chinese soil, especially when we went hungry ourselves.

Perhaps more damaging to the countryside was the rampaging poor who had turned to crime for their survival. Mom and I were stuck outside a burning town gate because the citizens of the town had started a fire thinking that we were bandits intent on robbing them. One of their lookouts had seen a man with a rifle in our truck and immediately thought the worst. The ancient stone wall that housed the burning wooden gate was so hot that water turned instantly to steam upon contact. We sat and waited for the stone to cool before we could drive through the opening.

Once we were inside this remote mountain-top town, the residents again piled firewood into the arched gateway. The mayor wanted us to stay. He even offered to house and feed us because the two soldiers traveling with us would be enough to scare off the bandits.

Unfortunately, this was not an isolated case in our journey. In the remote mountainous regions of southwestern China, law and order was essentially nonexistent.

When we reached Kweilin, Mom and I went to the Li River to spend a few days being tourists. This was the spot that Chinese watercolorists, calligraphers, and emperors visited to cleanse their heavily burdened minds. We spent that evening watching the sun set behind the wondrous limestone mountains that characterized its unique beauty. While the setting sun hid behind the bulbous mountains, the bright light-blue sky cast its majestic aura over our heads. Then, magically, as if a series of switches had been thrown, spots of lantern lights flickered on. Within minutes, dot after dot of tiny lights marched across the dark broad mirror of the Li River. Out there, the lantern-lit fishermen unleashed their cormorants on the unsuspecting fish.

We were reluctant to leave, but Mom had meetings to attend in Chungking. She was clearly upset and nervous. What do they want to talk to me about, she wondered. She didn't give me many of the details of those meetings because they had sworn her to secrecy. They had asked her not to publicly divulge her war-time experiences while under the employ of the Chinese Government. She even signed the equivalent of a non-disclosure agreement. She then made it clear to me that I was never to speak of our war experiences, too.

Though our lives had never been threatened, that unspoken danger was never far from her thoughts. Clearly, the wise thing to do would be to keep her silence.

After college, I asked her whether it would be permissible for me to tell our story. She said: "No." When I pointed out that the Chinese government of that era no longer existed, she said that a promise is a promise. But she gave me permission to tell our story after her death. Then she would smile and say: "I promise you this: I am determined to outlive all of my enemies."

By that, I knew she meant Chiang Kai-shek and Li Hanhun. Though neither one of these people had ever deliberately hurt her, she still considered them her enemies because of their inability to govern in a benevolent and generous way. Selflessness was not a word in their vocabularies. My mother believed that leaders should serve their constituents, not exploit and abuse them.

Chapter Six
Down the Mighty Yangtze

At the beginning of the war, our problem was getting out of Shanghai. At the end, it was getting back. Unfortunately, what we learned in Chungking was not encouraging or conducive to our return to Shanghai. The situation was actually a lot worse than it was before the war ended. Now that the Japanese were no longer in control, their disappearance created a social and political vacuum. Powerful local politicians and self-proclaimed warlords all claimed a right to rule their designated regions. The jockeying for power was in full force because the central command was disorganized and in disarray.

The Generalissimo's men were occupied with rounding up the Japanese. Many of his soldiers were stationed in the north trying to contain Mao Tse-tung and his band of ever-growing peasant soldiers. Chiang himself was occupied with re-establishing the Kuomintang (Nationalist) Government to a large portion of the country formerly held by the Japanese. And because the Party needed money, very often the highest bidder got the coveted position. Suddenly, a "warlord" became a "governor."

Left alone in the mountainous and remote regions were freely roaming bands of disgruntled, displaced peasants. They looted and pillaged the countryside for food and any valuables that they could carry, that is, if they couldn't eat it first. For them, there simply wasn't any other way to survive. These were landless people with absolutely nothing in their names.

One sure and ancient way for us to return to Shanghai was by boat down the Yangtze. Unfortunately, many remote stretches of the rugged and sparsely inhabited banks of the untamed, raging river were controlled by bandits. When possible, they stopped river traffic to collect a toll. And the obviously wealthy were taken and held for ransom.

But none of this deterred my mother. We went in search of a boatman who would take us to Shanghai. She had a number of leads. The most highly recommended one came from an American intelligence officer who worked with Uncle Jin.

The boatman that the American recommended had transported some top secret and sensitive documents through the Japanese lines from Chungking, down the Yangtze, to Shanghai.

Uncle Jin knew of him, but never met the man. He was known to be reliable. "Opportunistic, but reliable," was the cliché used to describe him. The next question was whether we could trust him with our lives, not just some secret papers.

Eventually, we found the man. His small junk couldn't have been more than twenty-five feet long. Its center section was covered with a semi-circular bamboo housing, the same design as the one on Uncle Wu's cargo junk. The housing constituted the main and only cabin on the junk. Braced against the front of the half-moon shaped cabin was a twenty-foot tall mast rigged with a traditional lug sail. On up-river journeys, this mast held the towrope.

We still had three gold coins and four rings left in my money belt. The jewelry included Mom's wedding band, her diamond engagement ring, a red ruby encased in a thick gold band and an 18-karat gold ring with a woven rope design. (Mom gave this ring to my wife, Jacquie, a few years ago.)

"Well, this must be it," Mom said. "I don't think the river pirates will pay too much attention to this junk, do you?" she said with a smile.

Just then a short stocky man in his forties came out of the cabin. He was dressed in faded black pants and shirt. He looked us over and raised his eyebrows.

We were dressed in nondescript peasant's clothing.

"Are you Mr. Ma?" Mom asked innocently.

The man smiled and nodded pleasantly at us. He had recognized us from Uncle Jin description.

Who can miss an attractive woman with her young son in tow. "And you must be Huang Tai-tai," he said respectfully.

Mr. Ma invited us aboard his vessel and served us tea. Formal introductions were over.

"Well, I was looking for something a little...a little more substantial than this..." Mom said affably, waving her hand at the junk. "Is this vessel safe?"

"Safe?" Ma burst out laughing. "I ran the Japanese blockade many, many times. And here I am," he smiled. "Even the pirates will not stop me. I am but a poor man," he said with a disarming smile. "They only rob the big fancy boats."

"And you know the river well?" Mom asked in her most innocent voice.

"All my life I am a river man. I know this river. I know every rock in every rapid by name. Many of my enemies have been led to a sad fate on some of those rocks. Those who dare to follow," he chuckled at his little private bit of bravado. "My little boat darts between the rocks like a dragon dancing on the waves," Ma waved his hand through the air as if his fingers were indeed dancing over the churning rapids.

"I see," Mom said with a bit of humor in her voice. "And when you're dancing between the rocks, how would you handle the bandits behind them?"

Mr. Ma grinned. "Why, like a dragon, of course. Like a fire-breathing dragon!"

"I like your wit, Mr. Ma. If you are as quick on the water as you are with your words, then you'll do. You'll do," Mom said with a smile.

"Huang Tai Tai, you honor me with such kind words," Ma replied with a bow of his head.

Mom slowly moved her right hand to her purse. "I will pay you two gold coins for the trip to Shanghai," she said casually.

Ma's eyes popped open with amazement. "Two coins will hardly feed me," he said, appearing to be appalled by this meager offer.

Mom looked taken aback by his reaction. "You did say that it would only take a few days to make the trip, didn't you? Two gold coins for a few days work, that's more than what a general makes," she declared.

"While it will only take a few days to go down river, it will take me a month to come back. How shall I live? What shall I eat? Will you ask a man to sacrifice his life to take you to Shanghai?" he pleaded with open palms.

Mom almost laughed but she suppressed it to a broad grin. "Oh, but Mr. Ma, these are my last coins. I have no more." Mom opened her small purse. There were only two gold coins in it. I had the other in my money belt. "You will have taken all I have. Isn't that enough?"

Ma shook his head dramatically from side to side. "Oh, no! No. It would not be right for me to take your last two coins," he said sadly as if it pained him to even think of such a thing. Then he brightened a bit as if an idea suddenly popped into his head: "Perhaps you have a relative in Shanghai who will pay me for my return trip?" he asked in a voice full of hope.

Mom bit her lips as if deep in thought. "I have not been in touch with my family since the war began. I do not know who is there. But, if I still have family there, I will ask them to pay you two more pieces of gold." Once again, Mom saw concern on the man's face. "Well, Mr. Ma, it won't be so bad to work in Shanghai, you know. They could always use a resourceful man like you," Mom quickly added. Then without another word, she gave him a letter from Jin.

Mr. Ma read the letter and his face suddenly brightened. That did it. Ma bowed twice in agreement. "OK," he said in English. "OK!"

⌒⟶

Captain Ma hoisted the heavy lug sail when the wind favored him especially along the calm broad sections of the Yangtze. A favorable wind generally meant a following wind that was no more than forty-five degrees off his stern. The hull of his river junk was shaped like the belly of a broad, fat fish, unlike Uncle Wu's cargo junk that had a flat bottom. The draft was deep enough to accommodate the forces of a following wind without tipping over, but shallow enough to bounce and skip atop the turbulent waves of the fast-flowing Yangtze.

This ancient and proven design allowed Captain Ma, and we called him Captain because it obviously pleased and flattered him, to use his long, double oars attached to each side of the junk as both a rudder and propeller. He expertly rode the river downstream very much as he had initially described it to us. His little junk danced and bobbed atop the water like a toy on a rushing stream as he furiously worked his oars to avoid the rocks. Our trip down the Yangtze can be likened to shooting the rapids on the most violent portions of the Colorado River, except that the Colorado rapids were tame by comparison. But the danger didn't deter these intrepid river men from using this violent artery as a major transportation route.

Captain Ma would not allow us to come out from under the cover during the day. He wanted to maintain the appearance of a sailor with his wife and son plying the river with no special purpose. He sailed stealthily during the day, stopping at strategic locations to check the safety of the next bend in the river. Seeing no danger beyond the bend, he would proceed.

"This river dragon is like a tempestuous woman," he said as he worked his oars to steer his little vessel between the rocks and through the churning rapids. "Look at how angry she gets when she's in a rage!" Mom and I held each other tightly as we rode down the rushing turbulence. It was both exhilarating and frightening at the same time.

The Yangtze River and its various tributaries crisscrossed the heart of China. It was, and still is, a vital artery for travel and commerce. Ma was one of hundreds of thousands of people who lived, worked and died on the river. People like him knew no other life. On land, they would be like fish out of water. How sad and yet how natural. People like him made commerce possible on this unpredictable body of water. Silently, we admired Ma's courage and expertise especially in the violent brown waters of the narrow gorges. His confidence was the only thing that kept us from panicking.

He saw the fear in our eyes as we approached our first major gorge. The Yangtze Gorges are monstrous when compared with the ones we encountered going up the North (Bei) River to Shaoguan.

"Ah," he sighed confidently, "do not worry, Huang Tai-tai. Think of the river as God's hand guiding this little boat through the alternating calm and strife of life. Just look at the beauty that surrounds you!" he exclaimed, his eyes darting between the upper reaches of the gorge and the clear blue sky above. "Look skyward and you will find peace," he pointed skyward to emphasize his point.

Our eyes peeled away from the churning and violent rapids. We looked at the top of the mountain gorges and lost sight of the violence on the river. Our sense of speed diminished because the sky and the mountains appeared to be stationary. From this perspective, Mom and I realized that we weren't going as fast as we had feared. From that moment on, we simply looked skyward for calm. We felt the boat under us, pitching and yawing and being thrown about, but we no longer felt the abject fear that the sight of this great untamed and rushing river elicited. Captain Ma had given us a rational way to combat our fear of the violent rapids.

When we reached Shanghai, the most striking sight was where the brown, silt infested water of the Yangtze met the blue-green ocean. There was a clear demarcation between the two colors. Mr. Ma explained that this is where the brown fresh water meets the sea.

When he docked his little boat at the Bund in Shanghai, a job was waiting for Captain Ma. He would handle special shipping assignments between Shanghai and Chungking.

The fighting had stopped, but the war was far from over.

Chapter Seven
Shanghai

Mom had been told to look for a driver standing by a jeep when we docked. He was easy to find because there was only one jeep parked at the dock. There was no one else there to meet us. I climbed in the back with our two bags while Mom sat in the front seat. The driver pulled away from the dock, one hand on the horn, the other on the wheel. He proceeded to speed down the Bund as if there were no other traffic on the road. There wasn't much car traffic, but the Bund was packed with pushcarts, rickshaws and pedestrians. Mom let out an audible gasp thinking that the jeep would run over these people, but magically, the sea of carts and people parted to let the jeep speed on. "Don't worry, Ma'am, I haven't hit anybody yet!" the driver said.

Mom was concerned that no one came to meet us until she discovered the only vehicle available to transport us was this little jeep.

The most reassuring thing about Grandpa's house was that nothing had changed. All of my uncles, aunts and cousins were there. They had survived the war in good health. Life went on as if the Japanese had never been here, at least on the surface. But Shanghai had changed, and not for the better. There were homeless refugees living on every street in the poorer neighborhoods. Only the old International sections of the city were spared. Every morning, death wagons would patrol the streets picking up lifeless bodies and hauling them away. To where? Nobody really wanted to know, only that they be removed to prevent the spread of disease.

The first and most important thing Mom wanted to do was to write to my father in New York. She wanted to start the process of getting a duplicate birth certificate for me. I would need it to get a new passport because she had destroyed all of the papers that linked us to America right after Pearl Harbor.

The second thing was to enroll me in a school. I couldn't adjust to the formal rituals of a Chinese school. It was much too strict. The students in the fourth grade behaved perfectly. They were obedient, orderly and studious. The teacher lectured and the students responded when called upon. No one ever spoke out of turn. I wasn't used to that. Besides, I was literally four years behind my classmates.

So, in self-defense, let me give you a hint of what it means to be a Chinese student learning the Chinese language.

The first thing you have to learn is how to hold a brush. Unlike a pen or pencil where you'd hold the pen at an angle, you have to learn how to hold the brush straight and perfectly perpendicular to the paper. To do this, you'd use your thumb, index and middle fingers. This position allows you to write a thin line by just using the very tip of the brush, and a thick line by pressing down on the tip. Using this up and down motion, you control the width of the ink on the page. This isn't as easy as it reads. Try it.

Now, you can start tracing Chinese characters on sheets of translucent rice paper. The words to be traced were printed on a page underneath. You copy each brush stroke perfectly, and copy them from left to right. And there was an order to each stroke. Some words have as many as twenty brush strokes. That meant you had to memorize the proper order of those twenty strokes, too. All of this was designed for righties. If you're a lefty, you have to use your right hand to write. It's a tough life for you lefties.

That's how you learn to write Chinese. You copy the characters over and over until you've painted each brush stroke perfectly. You're graded on how well you copy the words. Later, you're graded on how well you write in freehand, without copying. To become educated in writing Chinese, you had to spend years of your young life just copying. And you're talking about anywhere from 2,000 characters to 50,000 characters. The first would be enough for you to read the newspaper, and the second would make you a Mandarin.

Having suffered through this process, I can guess why so many Chinese are illiterate. Learning how to read and write was a full-time job. A farmer just doesn't have the time to sit every day and copy words for hours on end, not if he wanted food in his bowl. But what bothered me more is this: suppose you're not manually dexterous enough to handle a brush in this precise and demanding manner? Suppose you were born with a heavy hand where your large muscles were better developed than your small ones?

Surely, many people had been left behind in the Chinese educational system due to muscular development?

Though I had the physical ability to handle the brush properly, I couldn't catch up on the volume of work that I had missed. And I was considered to be a disruptive student because I didn't know that it was wrong to ask "why?"

My teachers sent notes home with me nearly every day. This disheartened both Mom and me. Clearly, the teachers didn't know how to deal with a boy who didn't know the rules of the game. And they didn't take the time to teach me the rules. They expected me to know them.

Thankfully, Mom ignored the reports of my absences. She knew we wouldn't be in Shanghai much longer. Still, she felt compelled to warn me about playing hooky on the streets of Shanghai.

"The streets are dirty, full of disease. People are dying of TB. They spit in the streets," she cautioned as she waved at the window. "You must be careful, you know!" she said sternly.

Other than the educated elite of China, everybody spat. It was both unhealthy and disgusting. (It would take a major re-educational effort by Mao Tes-tung and the Communist Party to stop this disgusting national habit. Today, nobody spits on the streets.)

"What do you do when you're not at school?" Mom asked with no recrimination in her voice or demeanor.

"This morning, I went to the market."

"Why did you go there?"

"There's a man who does magic tricks, and a strong man who breaks stones with his bare hands. They sing operas in a tent. There's a lot to see and do—and learn."

The market was an exciting place. But not a place for genteel folk. Located in the International section, it attracted the servants of the rich. Servants shopped there for their employers. Furthermore, this was an entertainment center for them. A place for them to relax, trade stories about their respective employers and just hang out during off-duty hours. Rarely did a servant get a full day off. I hung out with them. And nobody thought anything about a ten-year-old boy wandering around the marketplace. This was a common sight. The poor just can't afford school, not to mention the orphans who had to find way to survive. Children my age picking through garbage was an everyday, normal occurrence. If anything, I was the exception because I didn't have to scavenge.

"They have book stalls that rent all kinds of books. I read a few, too!" I told her. I wanted her to know that I was learning, but in a different way.

"Oh," Mom said as she raised her eyebrows. "What kind of books did you read?"

"Classical stories." There were pornographic books, but I didn't mention that, though I'm sure she knew.

Mom knew about these open-air bookshops. The classics I mentioned were pocketbook-sized with two black-and-white line illustrations on each page. The bookstall rented the books. The writing was simple but it was the pictures that told the story.

"You read comic books all day?"

"No, I explored. There's a lot to see. I learned how a moneychanger worked. The man used a hot fire to melt the gold. You should see how he does it. Then he'd pour the melted metal into a bucket of cold water. That's just how great grandfather must have found out about his fake coin, isn't it?"

"Yes, that is the traditional way. What else did you see?" she asked.

"I saw the opera. I liked the fight scenes. They danced with swords and lances. And they sang. Oh, there was an orchestra, too."

"An orchestra?"

"You know, drums and cymbals and strings."

"Which opera did you see?"

"It was about a king and his favorite concubine. She wanted to be his queen because she had given him a son. But the king still loved his queen, so the concubine killed her.

"And then bad things happened after that. The queen's father attacked because his favorite daughter had been killed."

"Did he really come to avenge his daughter, or did he come to conquer a new kingdom?"

"I don't know. The marriage made peace between the families, and then there was no reason for peace. They were fighting all the time during the time of the Warring States."

Mom flashed a surprised look on her face. "You know about the Warring States?"

I nodded.

"What else did you do?"

"Well, I walked a lot. There are lots of places to go. The other day I went to that ancient pagoda."

"That quite far isn't it?" she said with amazement in her voice.

"It was a nice walk. Not as long as those marches that I used to make with the soldiers."

"Did you learn anything about the pagoda?"

"Yes. A lot," I bragged to justify my actions. "The pagoda is a thousand years old, the monk told me."

"You talked with the monk?"

"Yes. He gave me lunch and tea."

"What did you talk about?"

"The war."

Mom looked at me and ran her gentle hand down my cheek. "What did you do with your lunch money? Did you give it to the monk?"

"No, he wouldn't take my money. He told me to spend it on good things."

"On good things? Such as?"

"I spent it on renting books. He told me it was all right to read the comic books. They told the history of China. He said that a good emperor is like the father of a big family. We should respect and honor him. But a bad emperor is not good and we should not obey nor honor him because he does not deserve it."

"You liked the monk, didn't you?"

"Yes. I like talking to him."

"I see. That's good," Mom said approvingly. "What else did you do?"

"I walked to the old city where Great Grandpa went. And I walked across the crooked bridge to the teahouse. Why is the bridge crooked?"

"Because evil spirits travel in straight lines, so they cannot cross the crooked bridge."

"Oh."

"What else have you seen?" Mom pressed on knowing that I had played hooky often.

I really didn't want to tell her for fear that she would stop me from exploring, but I changed my mind because I wanted to know why people did things like this. "I saw a dead baby on top of a garbage can."

Mom was visibly upset. "You did not touch it, did you?"

"I almost touched it. I thought someone had left a doll on top of the garbage can. It was so white. It

179

looked like a doll without any clothes. And it was fat, too."

"Go wash your hands," she said firmly.

"But I didn't touch it."

"Go on," she said shaking her head, "God knows what kind of germs you came in contact with!" She shoved me into the bathroom.

"But that was a few days ago," I protested.

"I don't care. Just wash your hands. Always wash your hands when you come home, understand! It does not hurt to be careful," she said as she stood over me.

I didn't argue because I knew how disease-infected the streets of Shanghai were. There were dead bodies everywhere. The cleanup crews couldn't keep up with the death rate. "Who would leave a dead baby in the garbage?" I asked.

"The baby probably belonged to a servant. She probably killed her daughter. It was a girl, was it not?"

I thought it was a doll because it didn't have anything between its legs. I nodded in reply.

"The mother probably could not afford to feed her or bury her. It is possible that her employer told her to get rid of the child or face dismissal."

"Why?"

"Because it is expensive to feed people."

"That's not right, is it?"

"No," she said. "But people are desperate. They will do anything to survive."

"Why is it all right to kill girls and not boys? Imagine if grandpa killed you, then I wouldn't be here, would I? You know what else? There aren't any women beggars, are there? All the beggars are men. Did they kill all the women?"

"In a way, I suppose they did. That dead baby you saw did not have a chance to become a beggar, did she?"

"No."

"Unfortunately, it is more complicated than that," Mom explained. "Women are not allowed to beg, you see. Ancient customs often do not make sense. Do you know why Chinese Emperors are all men? Or why men are the only ones who can become Mandarins and scholars? Did you know that all the famous women opera stars are really men playing a woman's role?"

"The women in the opera..."

"Yes," she said. "Are you surprised?"

I nodded.

"The reason that boys are more valuable than girls is that boys have a better future. Boys have more opportunities. Boys can become scholars, painters, writers, judges, policemen, governors...even women opera stars! Girls do not have those opportunities, so we are less valuable."

Mao and the Communists used the inequities between the sexes and between the rich and the poor to recruit people to their cause. Their movement was so successful that when they won the revolution in 1949, the poor people didn't hesitate to kill the wealthy. Mistreated servants turned on their employers and delighted in their slaughter. No mercy was shown simply because no mercy had ever been given.

"Come, sit down. There is something important I want to tell you. We are going to America," she announced softly, smiling.

"When? How?"

"As soon as I can arrange it," she said. "You are an American citizen, you know."

"I am?"

"Oh, yes. You were born in America. That makes you a citizen. We can go back to America to be with your father."

"I'm an American? Not Chinese?"

"You are both."

"Really? How come?"

"Well, if you are born in America you automatically become an American citizen," Mom said. "That is how all the people in America became citizens."

"Why didn't you tell me before?"

"I thought it was safer not to tell you. You see, the Japanese would have killed you if they knew."

"I would have kept the secret. Didn't I keep all our secrets?"

"Yes you did, and I am very proud of you. I don't know what I would have done if I didn't have you with me."

"We went through a lot, didn't we?"

"They were difficult years, but we made the best of it."

"Remember that time when we had nothing to eat all day but one egg? We couldn't even get a bowl of rice."

"Many people starved to death that year. We were lucky to get the egg. Life will be much better in America. The President promised that there would be a chicken in every pot!"

That was inconceivable. "What's America like?"

"The Chinese name for America is Mei Kuo, or literally, Beautiful Country. It is big, almost the same size as China. Shanghai is on the same latitude as New York. The two cities have about the same climate. And Canton is about where Miami is. That is why your grandfather calls Canton the Miami of China, you see. People in America live in their own houses and every family owns a car.

"Americans are the richest people on earth. They have all the natural resources. They have oil, coal, steel. They can make anything. In New York, they have the Empire State building. It is one hundred stories high!"

I really couldn't visualize such a tall building. My frame of reference was limited. It was enough that America was the only country that was capable of building such a building. Perhaps that's why today, nearly all former third-world countries want to build the tallest skyscraper in the world. It would be visual proof that they were no longer a poor, third-world country, but one on a par with the United States of America.

"Is it true that everybody in America sleeps on inner-spring mattresses?"

"Yes."

"All of them?"

"Yes, all of them," Mom said in a matter-of-fact voice.

The reason that I was so impressed by the idea of the inner spring mattress came from grandpa. He told me that at least a hundred coiled metal springs made up one mattress. To produce one million mattresses means that American industry had to make 100 million springs to put into those mattresses. Multiply 100 million people by 100 million springs and you have a mattress-making industry that's capable to producing 10,000,000,000,000,000 springs. The number was so big that I didn't know what to call it. And grandpa wouldn't tell me because he wanted me to learn it on my own.

"Do you know why Japan lost the war?" grandpa asked me. "If America can produce all those springs, how many bullets do you think they can make to kill the Japanese?"

Suddenly, I was proud to be a citizen of this powerful and wealthy country. "When can we go?"

"We have to get passports and visas. They say it will take a year for me to get a visa, and only if I bribe the right officials," Mom explained.

"And then we can go?"

"Yes," she said. "Now, you must not play hooky, do you understand? You must do your best to learn in school. You have to prepare for school in America, you know."

"But if I'm going to America, why do I have to learn Chinese?"

Mom laughed.

I continued to play hooky not in defiance of her wishes, but because Mom hadn't objected very strenuously. We both knew that learning how to read and write Chinese was going to be a waste of time. The coming challenge would be learning English. She already knew that we wouldn't be coming back to China anytime soon. Her tacit approval of my exploring Shanghai was a strong vote of confidence in my ability to take care of myself. This attitude boosted my self-confidence immeasurably. Moreover, she thought it would be better for me to be a street-smart kid than to be a book worm—which was most unlikely simply because I hadn't been exposed to books, yet. She knew what I needed to learn and it wasn't going to come from a classical Chinese education. She gave me the freedom to satisfy my curiosity.

Shanghai was a great place to explore. For the equivalent of a few pennies, I can see the old moving picture shows. You look into an eyepiece, turn a crank and watch a series of still photographs flip from one frame to the next. The people in the photos appear to move from frame to frame. Naturally, these moving picture shows were all pornographic. And the vendor didn't stop me from watching as long as I paid him the money.

The CARE packages from America used to contain these small sample packs of Camels or Lucky Strikes with three to four cigarettes in them. You could barter one of these sample packs for a bowl of hot noodles. It was the same with a Hershey's Chocolate bar. And if you were lucky enough to get a CARE package, you could live on it for a week. The poor scrambled for them. The crooks hijacked truck loads of them. And the bureaucrats routed them directly to their homes, right from the ship. Very few poor people got those life-saving packages.

The CARE packages were worth more than the yuan. They had real tangible value while the yuan was just printed paper that lost value everyday.

Once I came upon a long line of people. There was an open army truck parked at the head of the line. I asked someone what he was waiting for and he said that they were giving away loaves of bread. With nothing else to do, I decided to stand in line. I waited and waited, wondering why it was taking so long for the three men on the truck to give the bread away. Meanwhile, word had spread and the line grew longer. Finally, I looked up at the man standing on the tailgate. I asked for a loaf. He studied my face for a long moment, and then decided to grant me his largess as if he held my life in his hands. And for most of the starving poor in line, I think he did just that: people's lives were in his hands and he knew it.

During that hour or so, this small-minded bureaucrat must have felt like an all-powerful king giving bread to his poor starving people. And he had the arrogance and audacity to take his time to dispense the food. It was as if he wanted to lord it over us.

This loaf of uncut bread was as hard as a brick. God knows how long it had been sitting in the truck before the bureaucrats thought it was time to deliver it to the poor people of Shanghai. I couldn't even break the bread into chewable chunks. I walked away and discreetly handed the loaf to a dejected-looking little girl standing nearby. She had given up. She knew that by the time she got to the head of the line, all the bread would be gone.

I knew how she felt because I used to wait in line for the CARE packages. I didn't even get close to the truck before all the packages were gone. I would have had to get up at dawn to get in line to wait hours for a CARE package.

Today, I can envision this very same scene being repeated again and again around the world. It wasn't a pretty sight then, and it isn't a pretty sight now.

Men bought sex with cigarettes from the CARE packages. The trade was so blatant that a child could see it.

Once, out of curiosity, I tried to buy sex with a chocolate bar. The girl agreed and took the chocolate. I knew what to do from watching the peep shows but I was only ten years old and too young to do anything. The girl was my age. She enjoyed the chocolate. I enjoyed the experimentation, and maybe she did too. This was classic "You show me and I'll show you." (It would appear that this game is universal.)

While life was moving right along, every morning people showed up dead on the streets. The first time I saw a dead man on a Shanghai street, I thought he was asleep on the sidewalk.

By 1946, Shanghai had regained her stature as a shipping center. Incoming ships brought relief supplies from America, while outbound ships of all types and sizes were loaded with Japanese prisoners to be shipped home. At the end of the war, there were approximately 2,000,000 Japanese soldiers in China waiting to be shipped back to Japan.

One day, when Mom and I were walking to the Bund, we passed a large white Victorian-style mansion surrounded by a tall, black wrought-iron fence. A group of Japanese prisoners were sitting on the lawn. When they saw us, they rushed, en mass, to the fence. They were naked but for a white loincloth, like a sumo wrestler's mawashi It was a hot summer day. They waved and shouted at us.

"Buy my watch, cheap!" one shouted as he stuck his arm between the iron bars.

"Here! A gold ring!"

"Do not even look at them," Mom said. "They are disgusting. Like animals."

"What do they want?"

"They want to sell the watches and the rings that they stole. They want money, food and cigarettes. Do not look at them."

"How come they're here?"

"They are waiting to be shipped back to Japan. Shanghai does not have enough prisons."

"How come they don't wear any clothing?"

"That's their traditional loincloth. The Japanese are barbarians."

Mom lowered her head and walked away in obvious disgust.

What's significant is the fact that none of the captured Japanese soldiers were decapitated or slaughtered, en masse, after their surrender. China certainly had the opportunity, but not the will. We waited for the war-crimes trials to dispense Justice. But that is not to say that people didn't take vengeance into their own hands. I'm sure many Japanese soldiers were killed by angry vengeful citizens.

Meanwhile, the Chinese people are still waiting for a formal apology from the Japanese government for the Rape of Nanking. Japan's refusal to admit wrong-doing and the Chinese restraint from extracting vengeance is a telling reflection of the two societies.

For the Japanese to apologize would mean that they would have to admit that their soldiers behaved in a barbaric and dishonorable way in Nanking. This would be a near impossible thing for them to do because the Japanese think of themselves as a polite and proper society. They tend to defer to their superiors and they bow with respect to each other at every meeting. They are so polite and thoughtful that they don't count their change at a cash register. Why? The thinking is that if you count your change in front of the cashier, then you would be insulting him for not trusting in his ability to count. This would be an insult and a loss of face. After all, a cashier should know how to make correct change. He's paid to do that job.

The Japanese people are extremely sensitive to this kind of behavior because they fear that the person who has lost face would commit suicide. Consequently, they cannot believe that their soldiers would do such unspeakable things in Nanking. After all, it is the Samurai Code to uphold honor until death. There is no honor in massacring women, children and the helpless. A Samurai who violates his honor code must commit seppuku or ritual suicide. Consequently, to admit that they committed the massacre at Nanking would be to admit that they did a dishonorable thing. And, taken to its logical but extreme conclusion, the consequence of such an admission of dishonor would be to commit mass suicide. Clearly, this is something that they cannot do, and this is why Japan has not apologized.

It would be up to the newer generations of Japanese to make the necessary attitudinal changes to allow this to happen, but this is unlikely because the Rape of Nanking is not mentioned in Japanese textbooks. The Japanese simply cannot accept the fact that their soldiers had raped and pillaged Nanking.

With the resumption of commercial shipping, mail began to arrive at regular intervals from America. It had been nine years since Mom had heard from Dad.

"Your father said he's looking forward to seeing us. He wants us to send him a picture. He does not know what you look like, you know. You were just a baby when we came back to visit grandpa. We will have to get reacquainted with him. We will be starting a new life in America."

Once reliable mail delivery from America had been established, Mom began to get letters from my father. Invariably, there would be crisp new bills carefully folded between sheets of letter paper. Mom had requested tens and twenties because they were the preferred denominations for bribing Chinese officials. And we would need a steady supply of dollars to get our travel documents.

I treasured the envelopes with the cancelled American stamps on them. The really valuable ones were those that showed a clearly legible New York City postmark.

Each letter from my father meant that we were so much closer to leaving Shanghai. The city had become a frightening place. My mother would no longer take me out for a movie at night. The last time we went, a thief reached into the rickshaw and snatched her gold-framed glasses from her face. By the time she screamed and the rickshaw driver stopped, the thief had disappeared into the darkness.

Ever since that incident, Mom would clutch her handbag securely to her side. She instructed me to walk next to her with my arm touching her purse. That way no pickpocket could get at her money without first brushing me aside.

We always took a safe, less busy but longer route through the secure international section. Here, the streets were broad and clean and nearly deserted. The large estates that lined the wide boulevards were well maintained; the lawns sparkled like fields of green gems.

We finally exited the wide streets into downtown Shanghai. Ever cautious, she clutched her purse tighter against her body. People overwhelmed the sidewalk and overflowed onto the main thorough-fare, choking traffic. Drivers maneuvered their cars and trucks with one hand on the wheel and an impa-tient palm on the horn. Rickshaw drivers ignored the cacophony and made their way through the mass of bodies by following their own invisible path.

Mom led the way to an open plaza in front of the large white, Greco-Roman-style bank.

Moneychangers hovered about its grand white marble steps. They converged on her like prospectors after gold.

"Best price for American dollars!" they shouted as we approached.

"How much?" Mom said.

That was what they wanted to hear. The rush was on.

"How many dollars?"

"Twenty," Mom said.

"1,400,000," said one voice.

"1,450,000," said another.

With that quote, most of the moneychangers left.

"1,500,000."

"1,600,000." said a gambler. He knew that in a few days, it would reach that height.

That ended it. The winning bidder motioned to his subordinates. They brought over a suitcase. Mom inspected the bundle of neatly wrapped 10,000-yuan bills. Satisfied that she had received all 1,600,000 yuan, she gave the man her twenty-dollar bill.

Mom hailed a rickshaw and she securely wedged her bag of money between us. When we reached the old section of the city, she covered her mouth and nose with her handkerchief. She made me do the same because she didn't know whether the smell was raw sewage or rotting flesh. In either case, the air was not healthy to breathe.

We followed this routine whenever Mom needed Chinese money. The moneychangers in front of the bank gave better exchange rates than the official banking system.

The dollar and the British pound sterling were the only currencies that people wanted. She used to give me a 1,000-yuan note to buy an after-school snack. As the hyperinflation continued, my daily snack allowance increased to a 10,000-yuan bill a day.

Mom exchanged her U.S. Dollars for yuan only when absolutely necessary. American dollars were as good as gold.

⌒

The news article wasn't a long one, but it did include a picture of Governor-General Li and his family. "Well, look at this. Isn't this the same fellow you worked for?" grandpa asked.

Mom came around to her father's chair and looked at the picture. "Yes, that's him," she said in a subdued voice.

Grandpa looked up. Her tone of voice was a give-away. "Tell me about him. What kind of man is he?"

Mom hesitated. "Well, he was all right, I suppose."

"You haven't said a thing about him since your return. That's unlike you," grandpa said.

I started to say something, but Mom hushed me.

"I promised to keep certain information confidential," she said. "But I suppose it's all right for family members to know."

Grandpa looked at her with disbelief in his eyes. "What has this world come to if you can't even tell your own father about him, hey?"

Mom had wanted to tell grandpa, now his insistence opened the flood gates.

"Father, I was hesitant to tell you because I had promised not to say anything about the war. But I know this is simply nonsense. They are just trying to protect themselves and hide the truth."

"Hide? What is there to hide?"

"Well, I saw some documents that I wasn't supposed to see. They were bank statements from Switzerland—two numbered accounts. But don't worry father. Nobody knows that I saw them."

"Go on," grandpa said, leaning forward in his chair.

"Nobody knows about Chiang's participation in the scheme to move the gold from the Bank of Canton to numbered Swiss accounts. Outside of General Li, I'm the only one who saw those documents, but I have not told anyone that I saw them. And the general does not know that I saw them. As far as the world knows, the gold was never stolen. It just mysteriously disappeared. They claim that all the documents had disappeared in the chaos of war, too," Mom said.

"The money could have been used to fight the war—to buy arms and ammunition from the Americans. But they acted selfishly and sacrificed the country instead. I think what they have done is hateful," she said angrily. "Thousands of people died from starvation during the last year because of poor planning and stupidity. We couldn't even manage our own precious supply of gasoline. Li's security guard fell asleep and accidentally set the gas on fire. It was an accident that never should have happened. The man just didn't understand how flammable gasoline is. No one explained it to him. He warmed himself with an open brazier full of hot coals. It tipped over and the gas went up in a cloud of smoke. This was the man that Li put in charge of our gasoline!"

"You are certain that Li does not know that you saw the Swiss bank statements?"

"Yes," she said firmly. "The only way he would know is if I told him I saw them. As far as Li is concerned, nobody has seen those papers, except himself and his co-conspirators. His story is that nobody knows what happened. Bandits might have taken it during those last chaotic days. And of course Chiang went along with this story. They just wanted to keep the entire affair a secret, and they have. Who is going to contradict these two powerful men?"

"What about the Americans?"

"As far as they are concerned, this is an internal matter for the Chinese government. It is none of their business, but they know."

"Then why did they ask you to go to Chungking?"

"The Americans didn't ask me—Chiang, or rather, his staff asked me."

"Oh," grandpa said. "What did they want to know?"

"They were investigating the fire and they wanted to know if anyone had heard anything about the gold, or the anonymous letter that they had received. They were investigating the whole story. Naturally, the administration wanted to keep things quiet. Chiang's best response was to fire Governor Li before things got out of control. Before his own local party members rebelled against him. It was encouraging that he acted so quickly. Only it wasn't the corruption that did it. I think it was the gasoline explosion that finally ended Li's career. That explosion was not something that Li could hide. Especially when people found out that his own hand-picked guard had set the fire, and not a Japanese bomb.

"But Li told Chiang that the fire was an accident. So Chiang gave him the benefit of the doubt and a chance to save face. He suggested that Li take a leave of absence to do a diplomatic tour the world. Chiang told his friend that going abroad and studying the war-torn capitals would bring him respect and restore his luster. He told Li he could have his job back after his grand inspection tour. After he learned how other countries dealt with the aftermath of war, Li could apply his newfound knowledge to China. His newly acquired international credentials would enhance his position in Chiang's government."

"Unfortunately, that is the old Confucian way," grandpa said. "Education and then re-education can transform anyone. This also gives Li a chance to save face. It is certainly civilized of Chiang to let his friend off so easily. But then he has no choice, does he?" grandpa asked rhetorically. "Well, your former employer is about to leave on his face-saving world tour," grandpa said, angrily stabbing his finger at the picture in the newspaper.

"Madame Li has invited us to their bon voyage party," Mom said with a nod in my direction.

"They get to go before we do? That's unfair," I whined. "I'm an American citizen and they're not."

"I know. I know. But you do understand, don't you? This is how things are."

"You must go to their party," grandpa said. "Keep up the pretense. You will be fine, although I find it rather humorous that you have been sworn not to disclose the circumstances surrounding the fire."

"And the corruption by Li's cronies. They wanted to keep that a secret, too, but that didn't work because Chiang fired all of them, so everybody knew. And I was afraid that they had discovered my role in the secret meetings. Worse, I thought they knew I had somehow stumbled onto those secret Swiss accounts. Thank goodness it was none of those. Being a woman has its benefits. They always underestimate me. Perhaps the most ironic thing was the rumor that Madame Li circulated about me being related to Dr. Sun Yat-sen. When the rumor became as good as fact, it enhanced my reputation and it probably helped save our lives."

"You must not say anything to anyone about this, do you understand? This could be very dangerous for you and your mother," grandpa warned me.

"He understands, father."

"Of course he does! A boy who can walk past a Japanese guard with a money belt under his clothing can do anything. I am very proud of the both of you," grandpa said. "Now, tell me, how much longer will it take for you to get your visa to go to America?" Suddenly, grandpa wasn't so sure that we should stick around Shanghai much longer.

"A few more months, perhaps longer," Mom replied. "The corruption in Shanghai..." her voice trailed off. "Father, Chiang's government will not last long. We should sell our properties in Shanghai before the Communists take everything," Mom said hoping to get a positive reaction.

"I know the Americans," Grandpa said. "They will support Chiang, not the Communists. We will be all right. Besides, I cannot sell what my father left to me to hold and protect, you know that."

"But these are not ordinary times, father. I don't believe that Chiang will survive. Too many people are going over to the Communists. They are tired of the corruption. They are afraid of the total collapse of our economy. We are on the verge of going back to bartering to do business. The yuan is worthless. The Americans may say one thing in public, but in private, they think of Chiang as a little peanut. The Americans have no respect for him. They may support him with words, but they will not support him with their army."

"I have devoted my life to modernizing China, to build new infrastructure that will benefit the country for years to come. I will not abandon my principles. Regardless of who is in power, I will work with them to rebuild our country."

My great grandfather was illiterate. It is questionable whether his ancestral village even had a school. He learned everything from listening to people. His grocery stores were post offices and centers of communication. Returning workers from America told him how they laid mile after mile of railroad tracks over the Rockies and into the desert. About how the fire-breathing dragons slithered across the endless land that was America. They told of rail cars that carried people and freight across thousands of miles.

Mainly, they told of the riches that the fire dragons bestowed on Mei Kuo or Beautiful Country, the name that the Chinese coolies gave to America.

Though he had no formal education, he knew that China had once been the center of the world. In fact, the Chinese name for "China" is Tsong Kuo, or literally translated: Center Country. He saw China's River Dragons, the Yangtze and Yellow Rivers, as the country's lifeblood flowing across the land. Over two thousand years ago, the First Emperor completed the 1,100-mile Grand Canal that connected the southern city of Hangchow with the northern Imperial Capital of Peking. (Now Beijing) This north-south waterway helped control the floodwaters of the Yangtze and the Yellow Rivers. The Grand Canal was known as the bridle for the dragons. Additionally, grain from the south came up the canal to feed the northern cities. Commerce flowed freely over the River Dragons. China's wealth and commercial vitality came from these arteries.

Great grandfather Sun believed that China's waterways were similar to the great American railroads. When he compared China to America, he compared the speed of the steam locomotive, the fire dragon, with the snail's pace of the canal barge. He knew that China would have to change.

It was no accident that his number one son, Carlos, studied railroad engineering at Cornell.

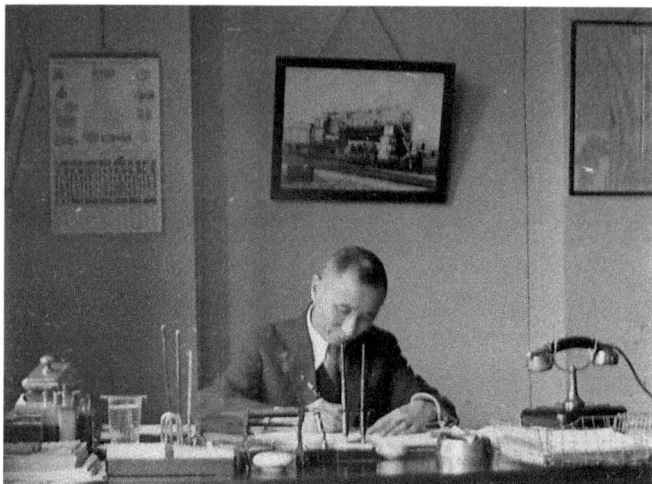

Carlos Sun at his office in Shanghai.

My Bou Bou was a tiny woman. Standing on her bound and mangled feet, she barely reached five feet. She came from a well-to-do family, one that was comparable to grandpa's. Her feet had been broken and bound in the traditional Chinese manner when she was a child. All of this pain and lifelong discomfort just to show society her status. She would never have to work and she would always be waited on. But times change.

When grandpa moved his family from our bombed-out compound to his town house in the city, there wasn't enough room to hold the family members and the staff. He had a staff of eight at the compound, but the town house could only accommodate three. The chef and his wife cooked for the family like they always did while the Amah took care of the children. After the move, the adults pretty much had to take care of themselves. Bou Bou was no longer waited on hand and foot.

Grandpa's house was a three-and-a-half storied structure. The kitchen and the servants' quarters occupied the ground level. The large French doors of the kitchen opened onto the backyard. There was a set of two, semi-circular stairways that wrapped themselves around the French doors. They were cantilevered over the doors and acted as a cover against the afternoon sun. The matching stairs curved down from the second floor to the garden. There was a wrought iron gate that opened out into the service road where the garbage cans were kept. It was on one of these service roads that I had seen the dead baby girl on top of a garbage can.

My cousins and I used to play in the walled-in garden. One hot afternoon, I was thirsty so I ran into the kitchen for a drink. Sitting on the work counter was a bowl of water. I picked it up and took a healthy gulp. Instantly, I gagged and spat out the rice wine. I couldn't spit out the remaining liquid in my mouth fast enough. Then I heard the heavy laughter. The chef had seen the whole thing. He ladled a cup of water into a bowl and handed it to me. I rinsed my mouth and then drank. I looked up at him with tears in my eyes. He gave me a spoonful of sweet black bean paste and told me to hold it in my mouth. The sweetness took the bitterness away.

From that day on, I used to go watch him prepare and cook dinner. On weekends, when he and his wife made dim sum for brunch, I would go watch them make the delicate dumplings and assorted delicacies. Because I took such an interest in their work, they would take the time to teach me how to prepare and cook. I've been cooking ever since. It was better than playing hooky.

Upstairs, Bou Bou used to play a game with me. When I did something good or said something funny that pleased her, she'd stop whatever she was doing and hold her finger to her lips. "Shhhh," she'd say. "Don't tell anybody, but come into Bou Bou's room in two minutes. I have a surprise for you." Then she'd glide off on her tiny bound feet like an angel walking on air.

Naturally, I couldn't wait the two minutes, so I followed her. Her door was slightly ajar. Bou Bou had a box of chocolates hidden on top of her bureau—just high enough and out of my reach. She took a chocolate out of the box then replaced the box.

"You may come in now," she said in her small sing-song voice.

"Which hand," she'd ask, holding out both arms.

If I guessed wrong, she'd squeal with delight and show me the chocolate in her other hand. If I guessed correctly, she'd frown as if she had lost the game. In either event, she'd give me the chocolate.

One afternoon, I hadn't seen her that day, so I went looking for her, hoping to play her game. Her bedroom door was slightly ajar. I peeked in. She was sitting in her chair with her left foot resting on a small low stool. She had taken off her tiny silk shoe and was in the process of unwrapping the gauze bandage from around her foot, something that her maid used to do. She was having a difficult time of it because it was hard for her to bend her back. She couldn't hold that bent position for long. She'd unwrap one round, then sit back and rest. Then do it again, each time with obvious discomfort.

Having seen enough, I walked into her room, silently sat down on the floor next to her stool and began unwrapping her bandage. She didn't say a word.

Her foot had been broken at the arch, and her malformed toes had been bent under her foot. In effect, she was walking on her shriveled-up toes.

I looked up at her. "Slide that basin over here," she said softly. "Use the cloth to wash my foot."

"Does it hurt, Bou Bou?"

"No, but it smells if I don't wash it," she said with a laugh. She gave me a towel. I dried her foot. "Here's some scent. Rub it on, then you can bandage me again."

Former Governor Li, his wife, two daughters, two sons, one interpreter and the children's Amah left China in January, 1947. They traveled First Class on their way to their first stop, America.

We saw them off and wished them well.

The Li's got an apartment on the West Side of Manhattan. Once their children had been enrolled into the proper schools, the former governor and his wife left on their global tour. First they visited Europe, then South America.

Li was getting his international credentials in preparation for his return to Chiang's government. True to the Confucian tradition, education would cure all past transgressions. Knowledge equals enlightenment, even for the worst of the sinners. (The ardent revolutionary, Mao Tse-tung, believed in re-education as a means of rehabilitation. This practice still goes on in China today.)

Meanwhile, the political situation China was deteriorating. Chairman Mao's Army was growing by the day.

⌒‿⟶

The YWCA in Shanghai was a large block of a building built from yellowish-gold slabs of stone. The four-story structure included a square walled-in courtyard guarded by a massive black, wrought iron gate. The concrete courtyard had a number of parking spaces, but the gates were shut and the yard was not used for parking anymore. A shortage of gas meant few cars. And in keeping with the symmetry of the structure, a balcony on the second floor matched the width of the front steps below.

A large covered well was located just to the right of the main entrance.

When the job as Director of the YWCA became available, Mom took it. She wanted and needed to do something while waiting and bribing her way through the Passport-visa process. She took the job to assert her independence and to show her father that she was, indeed, one of the new generations of Chinese women. The Sun family had been advocates of modernization since the nineteenth century. She wanted to continue the family tradition.

Mom and I occupied a two-room suite on the second floor of the YWCA. Our two windows looked down squarely at the well below. There were no bathrooms in the building. A neat row of stone bath stalls had been built behind the building, and a row of toilets had been placed some distance behind them. This was a woman's residence. The only other male was the caretaker. As there was no running water in the old building, the caretaker's main function was to bring water from the well to the kitchen and to the bath stalls.

I slept in the room with the windows overlooking the courtyard, directly above the well. One night, the sound of water splashing woke me up. Knowing that something was wrong, I woke Mom. She had heard the splashing sounds, too. She opened the window and shouted: "Who's there?"

The splashing slowed and a small voice answered: "It's only me," the caretaker responded sheepishly.

"What are you doing down there in the middle of the night?"

There was silence for a long time. "I...I fell in."

"Oh my God," Mom said.

"I'm sorry I woke you ma'am. I didn't want to disturb anyone with my foolishness," he said.

Mom rushed downstairs turning on the outside lights as she went. The bucket was in the well. "Grab the bucket," she shouted.

"Yes, ma'am."

"Grab the rope," she told me, "let us try to pull him up." We pulled, but he was too heavy. "Go get help, wake some of the women."

I ran into the building.

"Hold on to the bucket until help comes."

"Yes, ma'am."

The women arrived and we pulled him from the well.

"What happened?" someone asked.

"I was getting water for the kitchen, like I always do, but I slipped and fell in." The caretaker hung his head in shame.

"It is all right," Mom told him, "accidents do happen. Now go dry yourself." Then she turned to the rest of the people: "He's fine. He's fine," she said as she waved everyone inside.

The poor man had been willing to stay in the well until daylight just so he wouldn't wake anyone. Mom realized how prevalent this sense of deference was with the average Chinese. This was being polite and considerate to the extreme, but that was the mentality promoted by the Confucian ideal. The lower the class, the more deference and politeness one showed, regardless of gender. And this was the Confucian social order—all the way up to the Emperor. The pecking order was clear. You always deferred to and obeyed the rank above you. Women deferred to men, because men ranked above women. Wives deferred to husbands. But having lived in America gave Mom a different perspective.

Mom was clearly annoyed at the caretaker for being so meek and subservient, but she couldn't reprimand him for being who he was. Instead, she told him that everyone at the Y counted on him. That the Y wouldn't have water for cooking, cleaning and bathing were it not for him. She told him how important he was to the organization—the Y couldn't function without him. She tried to instill a new sense of self worth in him, and as a consequence, he became even more productive. No one had ever empowered him like this before. His new-found sense of confidence actually expanded his horizon and made him a bigger contributor to the organization. For the first time in his life, he had been told that he was important and that he had value. While he still drew water from the well to supply the needs of fifty people, he was now conscious of his contributions. He was no longer just a mule that hauled 50-pound buckets of water to the kitchen and the baths.

Mom also encouraged him to expand his skills and duties, knowing that he would, one day, be replaced by a few pipes and a pump.

On Sunday evenings, the Y's courtyard was turned into an outdoor movie theater. News footage from the United States about the war against the

Germans and the Japanese were shown to overflowing crowds. The people of Shanghai saw the atomic bomb explode over Hiroshima and Nagasaki. And when the Japanese signed the unconditional surrender on the Battleship Missouri, the crowd cheered even though that was old news. But the people turned silent when they saw the liberation of the German concentration camps and heard the horrible tale of the mass murder of millions of Jews. The sight of those starved skeletal bodies with deep, blank sunken eyes told a horrifying story. But everything was all right now. America had saved the world. No one doubted or disputed it. Everyone in China knew it. Even the Communists.

We all hoped that the world was now a better place.

It was clear that America had fought the war for Freedom, while the Japanese had fought for loot and booty.

Meanwhile, Mao's Communist revolution was gaining strength and pace. Mom knew we had to leave as soon as possible. Generalissimo Chiang Kai-shek was going to lose this war, too. The fact of the matter is that the Generalissimo hadn't ever won a major battle against the Japanese. Why would the war against the Communists be any different?

Mom developed a carefully planned ritual whenever we went to see a government official about our travel documents. She would wedge a small envelope into her purse, then make certain that she could take this envelope out easily, even without looking. She practiced until she was comfortable with the procedure. She had set things up so that there would be no fumbling around with her purse to get the envelope. She wanted to do it smoothly to impress the bureaucrat with her business-like efficiency. And as a safety measure against pickpockets, she closed the flap to her purse, hung the leather strap on her shoulder then tucked the black bag securely beneath her armpit. As always, she made sure that I walked next to her purse.

She hailed a rickshaw and haggled with the coolie over the price of the ride. This ritual sometimes ended up with her going to another rickshaw in search of a better price. There was never any hurry in these small financial negotiations. It was part of the cultural process back then to negotiate to get the best price. One rickshaw driver might value his time differently from another. The price a rickshaw man charged is totally under his control. He can sell himself cheap or dear, depending on his circumstance of the moment. If his belly were full, then he might want to charge more because he's not desperate for food. Conversely, if he's hungry, then he might be willing to charge less just to get the job so he can eat. This is the classic Chinese supply-and-demand, labor-intensive economy. When in China, you negotiate because each person sets his own value for his time.

And take your time. Life should be leisurely. In the old days, no one in Shanghai was ever on time. There was a social stigma to showing up on time for any function.

This tradition took form in early Imperial times. The emperor always showed up late for his appoint-ments. Naturally, no one dared to comment on his lateness. After all, he was the emperor. He could do as he pleased. In time, other important members of the Court began to follow the emperor's lead. No socially-aware person criticized this practice because it would have meant being critical of a superior's behavior. With time, this practice trickled down the ranks until it became socially acceptable with the upper crust and finally among the wealthy middle class. The tradition flourished as a status symbol. Being late was both fashionable and a statement of your social position.

The bureaucrat kept us waiting for forty-five min-utes, even though we had arrived late. Obviously, this man held an important position because he was so busy that he could keep us waiting for as long as he wanted. At least that was the unspoken message he wanted to convey. This was a standard tactic because the payoffs got bigger as you went up the line. Finally, the bureaucrat welcomed us into his office.

"Please, have a seat," he said with a polite bow.

"Thank you, sir," Mom said respectfully as she sat down.

The bureaucrat sat down after he saw that Mom and I had taken our seats. He smiled as he picked up his lit cigarette from the ashtray. He took a drag as he studied the papers on his desk. The genial-looking civil servant glanced up from a file folder and flashed an insincere smile. He leaned back in his chair then tapped his cigarette in the ashtray. "Ah, let me see," he said coyly, "you and your son wish to go to America, is that not so?"

Mom nodded and smiled warmly at him. "My son is an American citizen, you know," she said with a hint of pride. "According to American law, the mother of an American citizen has the right to accompany her under-aged son to the United States."

The bureaucrat smiled benignly at her, nodding his head as she spoke. "Yes, yes. You are one of the lucky ones," he said with a hint of impatience. "Do you realize how many applicants we have?" He pointed at a long row of four-drawer, gray-metal file cabinets against the wall. He leaned forward for emphasis. "Hundreds of thousands!" he lied. "Yes, that many. It would appear that all of China wants to go to America." He sat back. He wasn't smiling anymore. "Clearly, that is impossible, is it not, Madame?" He did not utter Mom's name though it was right in front of him. Using her name would have meant that she was an individual, and he wasn't ready, as yet, to recognize her in that particular way.

"Of course," Mom agreed somberly. Judging from his strident tone, she wondered whether she had brought enough of a bribe.

The man shifted in his chair as he dragged on his cigarette. He exhaled and blew two thick columns of blue smoke through his nostrils. The civil servant lifted then dropped his pack of Camels in an impatient manner. At that time, a pack of American cigarettes was better than Chinese money. People used it as currency. Mom understood the significance of those cigarettes. "Now, then, considering our backlog, how may we help you?"

"Ah, you are so kind for asking, Mr. Director," Mom said obsequiously. She made a minor event out of opening the flap to her purse, then looked up at him and smiled. "My husband is in New York," she said as she reached into her wallet and removed the letter that she had so carefully placed there. "He has written you a personal appeal. I believe it would be worth your while to read this." She leaned forward, the envelope clasped delicately between two fingers.

"Ah, so," the bureaucrat said with interest. He dropped his pack of cigarettes for the last time.

He took the envelope and opened the flap as he sat back in his chair. He blinked at the small portrait of President Jackson. That was all he needed to see. He opened his drawer and tucked the envelope inside. Slowly, deliberately, he slid the drawer shut.

Mom nervously watched his every move.

The bureaucrat reached across his desk, picked up a rubber stamp and pressed it firmly on the black ink pad. His deft fingers moved like a money-counter's as he flipped officiously through a series of pages, stamping each page in rapid succession as he did so. Then, as if it were beneath him to look directly at her, or because he felt some slight sense of guilt, he held out the papers to her.

Mom reached over and took it. She quickly studied the pages, knowing that to do so in front of him is an insult to his integrity. But she didn't care because she had paid dearly for them. The niceties of normal social behavior no longer applied. Mom looked up and smiled.

"Thank you," she said, after making certain that all the appropriate pages had been stamped. He didn't look happy at her performance. He knew Mom had insulted him on purpose.

It had taken her about a year to get permission from the Chinese government to leave the country. During that time, the bureaucracy moved her file from one civil servant's office to another. Each time she had to give the new civil servant money. And it was always in American dollars. At first, she gave dollar bills just to get the proper forms. And as she went up the bureaucratic chain, the bribes became more expensive. Ten dollars was equivalent to roughly two weeks' salary for some civil servants. With each step along the way, she had been assured that progress was being made. The procedure was complex they told her. We went there nearly every other week to follow the path of our papers, leaving a trail of dollars behind.

She often wondered whether the money she had spent would make a difference, or whether they would deny her permission anyway. There was no telling what these government officials might do. What if they claimed to have lost the papers? She had heard such horror stories. People had to start all over again.

Fortunately, Mom had been smart from the start. From day one, Mom used American money. She wanted to establish a reputation. In time, the bureaucrats expected dollars from her. Consequently, her papers exchanged more hands than was necessary. While this procedure cost more, it also guaranteed progress. Everybody got a piece of the action.

That's how the government worked in China.

⌒➤

My granduncle's house, or better yet, residence, was a huge courtyard home. There were three large, independent structures designed along the traditional Chinese lines with the curved roofs and glazed-roof tiles. The compound looked like three smaller structures from the Forbidden City had been moved and plunked down in the middle of Shanghai. In the center of two of the buildings was a square, formal garden. There was a goldfish pond fed by a running brook; various and numerous exotic plants and trees; and one octagonal gazebo with a jade-green roof. Under the center of this roof was a large, round white marble table capable of seating twelve people.

My granduncle wanted to treat me to a special Sunday brunch—just the two of us.

It was a warm spring day and a soft breeze danced its way between the green columns of the gazebo. Tea was served first in a glazed green teapot—and green cups—both designed to match the green tiles of the gazebo roof.

We sat opposite each other. He was a rotund man who obviously enjoyed food. This was probably why he ran the food portion of the grocery business, while my grandfather ran the real estate portion. This division of labor suited both men. The two brothers got along extremely well. The only thing that separated the two of them was their individual lifestyles. Grandpa was a practical engineer, while granduncle was a larger-than-life salesman with a touch of the showman brimming around his waist. His banquets were famous and usually bigger than anyone else's.

And then the servants proceeded to serve dumplings, or dim sum, in small white porcelain plates. Naturally, they matched the white marble table. There were thirty varieties of dumplings, three to a plate. It took the chef and his three helpers all morning to prepare the brunch.

Most of this food went uneaten. My granduncle didn't want me to forget him or Chinese food while I was in America. He told me that I would most likely never see the likes of such a spread again. And I haven't.

The night before our departure for America, grandpa took the whole family, his children and grandchildren, out to dinner. Dinner for eleven people cost two large suitcases packed full of large denomination bills. The owner of the restaurant didn't even bother to count the money. He just counted the bundles of bills. That's how absurd life was in Shanghai.

Chapter Eight
America

Mom had booked passage to America on one of the ships in the President Line, the General Gordon. The last time we saw this ship had been at the Li's bon voyage party. They had occupied a spacious suite on the upper deck of the luxury liner. Now, anchored in Shanghai bay, the ship once again received its passengers from motorized junks. Large luxury junks ferried the first-class passengers to a grand stairway that angled up to the promenade deck. Small ordinary junks shipped the steerage passengers to a big black gaping hole that was ten feet or so above the waterline of the ship.

The junk bobbed up and down in the waves as two crew members, one on each side of Mom, held her by the arms and hoisted her onto the teak platform at the foot of the ladder. Then the sailors hoisted me over. We climbed the short angled stairway onto the ship. Bits and pieces of lettuce, cabbage and broken eggshells littered the steerage reception area. The stink of wet rotten garbage wafted from the steel deck. Mom wasn't sure whether this was where the ship discharged its garbage or took on its fresh food supplies. Anyway, it really didn't matter. What was important was not the accommodations, but that she had found a way for us to leave.

The ship's crew tossed our bags onto the wet, filthy metal deck. Large wet stains mingled with bits of lettuce stuck to the leather. We picked up our belongings and followed the directions of the American crew. They inspected the green, four-by-five tag that hung around each passenger's neck. They pointed us to the forward section of the ship. Mom led me down the dark, dank passageway. Gradually, the damp smell disappeared only to be replaced by the odor of human bodies. The smell reminded me of the gym at the Y.

The forward cargo hold was a large cavernous space that had been outfitted with bunk beds stacked four deep. Two stacks were mounted side by side with khaki canvas separators between them. Row after row of these bunks stretched across the hold. Two people could pass each other on the narrow aisles but only if both turned sideways, and even then it was a squeeze. This luxury liner had been converted into a troop ship during the war. Now, the shipping company used its carrying capacity to haul Chinese immigrants.

"Come on, Mom! Let's go upstairs," I said the moment we had located our bunks.

"Let's put our things away first," she said.

"Do we have to?"

She glanced around pointedly at our surroundings and I knew what she meant. Mom unpacked our clothing and placed them into our assigned footlockers under the bottom bunk. Then she stored and locked her valuables in the metal lockers that lined the walls. She made sure that her belongings were secure before we went topside.

The first things Mom bought at the concession stand were two bottles of Coca-Cola and a bright yellow pack of Juicy Fruit chewing gum.

"You are supposed to chew this candy, not swallow it," she told me. She wanted to introduce me to the American way of life immediately and in the most pleasant way possible.

We walked out onto the forward deck and stood by the railing. Shanghai was just a half a mile away. I went to the tip of the bow and looked through the holes that the anchor chains pierced. It was a long way down to the water.

"Hey, get away from there," an American sailor shouted.

I didn't understand what the man said, but I bolted at the harshness of his voice.

The sailor had a fire hose in his hands and he was preparing to wash down the anchor chains as they were winched aboard. Just then, a junk floated alongside the railing where some steerage passengers stood. A wicker basket attached to the end of a twenty-five-foot long bamboo pole waved in the air. The small junk bobbed and pitched in the water, but the man was able to keep his bamboo pole steady and the basket of goods a few feet from the passengers on deck. Mom waved away the basket full of trinkets and postcards. Not to be deterred, he persisted.

"It's only a few pennies for a post card, ma'am. What's a few pennies to a rich lady like you?" the salesman said. Anyone going to America was, by definition, rich

Mom turned away. The seaborne merchant continued to hawk his wares to another passenger. There were no buyers.

The American sailor saw what was happening and suddenly, he turned on the hose and shot a plume of water at the merchant. The man staggered from the force of the blow. He danced atop the high aft cabin of his boat trying to regain his balance and, at the same time, keep his merchandise from going overboard. "Dew naa ma goor hay," he cursed when his feet were firmly on deck.

"Fuck your mother's cunt, yourself," the American sailor hurled the Chinese curse back at the man. The sailor hit him with another burst of water. This time the merchant was prepared for it. He dodged aside and quickly handed his bamboo pole to his wife. The merchant cupped his genitals with both hands and thrust his hips in the sailor's direction. "Fuck your mother's cunt with this!" he yelled. "Dew naa ma goor hay" was the coolies' favorite curse words in China.

Embarrassed by this performance, Mom grabbed me and led me away.

"The man is only trying to make a living," Mom said in clear crisp perfect English, "leave him alone."

The sailor looked around, unable to determine where those words came from or who said them. Puzzled and shocked by the emotionless Chinese faces around him, he did as he was told, glancing guiltily about as he returned to washing the salt from the ship's anchor chains.

"Why is that man so mean?" I asked.

"That is the way some people are. Do not pay any attention to him. This is our last day here. Let us begin our new life joyfully, shall we?" she said.

"How about another Coke, Mom?" I responded opportunistically.

"O.K.!" she said enthusiastically.

We spent most of our time above decks. Mom was really disappointed that we were in steerage. But a ticket to America was hard to get. You get what you can, when you can. Everyone wanted to go to the land of the free and the home of the brave. We were one of the lucky ones. Apparently, only the super rich, the well-connected, or high government officials could get private cabins on these trans-pacific crossings.

Photograph of bearer

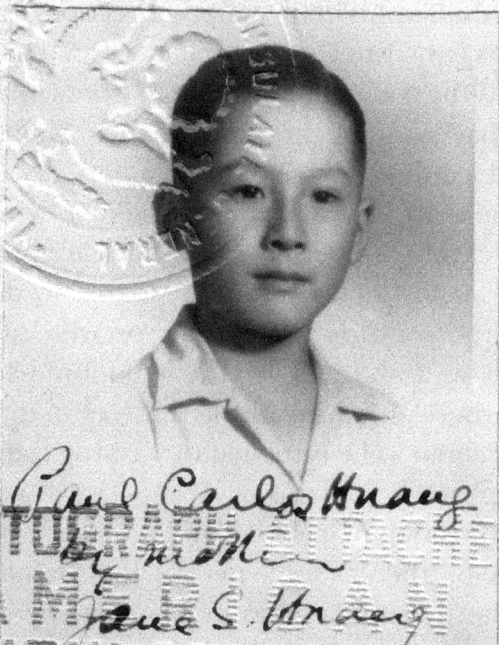

PHOTOGRAPH ATTACHED
A M E R I C A N
CONSULAR SERVICE

U.S. IMMIGRATION SERVICE
ADMITTED
MAY 16 1947
ADMITTED
PORT OF SAN FRANCISCO

*The author at age 10. I didn't know
how to sign my name in English.*

The ship's first port of call was Yokohama, Japan. The General Gordon docked and the crew unloaded cargo for the American occupation troops. On the gray concrete dock below, Japanese workers scurried about with straw sandals on their feet and a diaper-like loincloth around their crotches. They each wore a white towel around their foreheads. The towels draped over their shoulders thus protecting their bare backs against the wooden crates. The endless human chain of near-naked workers looked like a determined column of ants set on storing their winter's supply. Mom and I watched them work and she begrudgingly gave them credit for their teamwork.

"See how they work together? They keep the same distance from each other, and they walk at the same pace. Not like the Chinese dock coolies who work at their own pace. The Japanese work like machines. No wonder they were so good at war," she said.

The ship's crew laid the cargo net flat on the deck and loaded the center of it with supplies. The winch operator pulled a lever and the net moved up and wrapped itself around a tall pallet of wooden crates. Slowly, the overloaded net separated from the ship's deck. The operator pushed a long yellow handle and the boom swung the cargo to the dock. Suddenly the clacking winch stopped and the boom jerked to a halt. The abrupt stop caused one of the wooden crates above the netting to tip onto its side and its momentum carried it into the air.

"Oh!" Mom exclaimed as her eyes darted between the falling crate and the dockworkers below. The wood splintered on impact and the glass bottles inside fractured into small sharp shards. A puddle of brown liquid appeared on the gray concrete. For an instant, the dockworkers stood frozen in place, uncertain of what had happened. Then, as if someone had given a signal, the men unhooked their metal drinking cups from their loincloths, converged on the puddle, dropped to their haunches and began feverishly scooping the liquid into their cups. They drank with total disregard for the broken glass.

"What are they drinking, Mom?"

"Whiskey," she said. She didn't feel sorry for our former enemies. She knew that the American occupation forces treated the Japanese with dignity and generosity. America gave these people jobs and fed them instead of looting their food and valuables. The U.S. government supported the Japanese currency and tried to create a working economy.

"Those supplies came from America," Mom explained. "The Americans are not treating the

Japanese like slaves...like the way the Japanese treated us."

(When we returned to Shanghai after the war, Mom's steamer trunk full of antique scrolls had been confiscated. Her inheritance was gone. And grandpa's favorite working, miniature steam locomotive along with his collection of Ming Dynasty porcelain had been confiscated as well. I wonder how many of our antiques are decorating Japanese homes today.)

The sight of the Japanese scurrying about desperately scooping up the liquid seemed only fair. In a way, it was closure to see our former conquerors demeaned to such a degree.

We turned our backs on the scene and walked away.

We had lived in fear of the Japanese for ten years. The pitiful sight of these once mighty conquerors scurrying like animals for a taste of the good life seemed appropriate.

For me, it was a just way to end WW II. But not for my Mom. For the remainder of her life, she refused to buy anything made in Japan. She wasn't going to support their way of life.

In 1949, the Communists took China and Chiang Kai-shek fled to Taiwan with the remainder of his army and his friends and supporters. My grand uncle was one of them. Towards the end, entire armies switched sides and went over to the Communists.

In that same year, grandpa gave all of his properties to the People's Republic of China. The ones in Shanghai and his winter home in Canton. Since his railroad had been nationalized, his stock was now worthless, so there was nothing more to give.

However, the new government was gracious enough to let grandpa live in his house. The Chef, his wife and our old Amah wanted to stay in grandpa's employ. They had been with the Sun family most of their lives and now there were no jobs for them to go to and no place to live. The Communist Party agreed to let them stay because they wanted grandpa to continue to manage the railroad. They had no one who was qualified to do the job. When he retired, the government paid him a pension. They also paid pensions to the three who stayed.

Both grandpa and Bou Bou died peacefully of old age.

After their deaths, his house was converted into apartments. Until recently, my Sixth Aunt lived in one of them to maintain some semblance of our past ownership. There was a time when we thought we might get our properties back, but that hope has long been buried beneath the new high-rises of Shanghai.

⌐⟶

The former Governor-General Li and his family stayed in New York. Chiang did not give Li his old job back. Taiwan was too small for the both of them. In the end, Li's global tour benefited no one.

In 1951, Mr. and Mrs. Li opened a Chinese restaurant in the Bronx, but not without some controversy. A number of immigrant businessmen in Chinatown thought that the famous Governor-General would have an unfair advantage over other Chinese restaurants in the area. They thought that the Governor should go into some other business and not compete against ordinary, less-famous immigrants struggling for a living. The Chinatown newspapers covered the story, but the protests did not stop the Li's.

Mom and I were invited to the opening, but we didn't go. Mom didn't want to see them. She had too many bad memories.

"Interesting, isn't it," she observed. "Here's a man who has had no visible means of support for the last six years, who suddenly has to open a Chinese restaurant to survive. How poetic."

⌐⟶

One of Mom's ambitions was to "outlive all of her enemies."

This, I believe, she did.

Unfortunately, we lost track of our good friends Uncle Jin and Auntie May after 1947. I hope they outlived all of their enemies, too.

Jane Sun Huang died April 23, 2012 at the age of 99. She was just six months shy of her targeted and magical century mark.

She kept her promise not to reveal her experiences of World War II during her lifetime. Just as I had promised that I would honor her request to tell her story after her death.

I believe my mother lived a courageous, moral, and meaningful life. I hope this little book is worthy of her.

On a personal note, I've had a difficult time writing this book because it's been hard for me to reveal myself. It's been an emotional struggle simply because I had been trained to keep secrets at a very early age. Consequently, I'm more than reticent to talk about myself or my family. While I'm fully aware of this, it still has not been easy to tell all. But, I hope I have revealed enough to make my mother's story an interesting and satisfying read.

Acknowledgements

I would like to thank my good friend George Golfinopoulos for his insightful editorial comments. Who would have thought that a lawyer would make a good editor? Thank you George.

Thanks, too, to Bob Sherman, a wonderful, kind, gentle artist and designer, who created the maps and restored the old photos used in this book. His selfless heart is big enough to tackle a job so much beneath his talents that it leaves me in awe of him. Thanks for your generous soul, Bob

And, there's Harry and B.J. Hill and Nancy and Dennis Dowd who read an earlier version of the book and who's comments and encouragement helped me finish my work.

Finally, there's Jacquie, my wife. Her loving encouragement and helpful comments through innumerable drafts made this book possible. I could say more, but that would mean another book. Thank you, Jacquie!

Author Biography

Paul C. Huang is a writer-creator-entrepreneur who is featured in the twenty-seventh edition of *Who's Who in the East* and the first edition of *Who's Who in the Media and Communications*. His work as writer-producer-director on the documentary film *Chinatown, Inc* won him a bronze medal in the 1977 International Film & Television Festival of New York, an award he received again, a year later, for his work on *Billions for Defense*.

Huang is the creator of the *Dynasty Game*. He authored two cookbooks, *The Illustrated Step-by-Step Chinese Cookbook* and *The Illustrated Step-by-Step Beginner's Cookbook*, and is coauthor of a high-school textbook. His most recent title, *Escape from Shanghai*, is a memoir about the secret, revolutionary life of his mother—a true story that's more compelling than most fiction.

Huang currently lives in Florida with his wife Jacquie. He is the former chief operating officer of Tribeca Interactive, a division of Robert De Niro's motion picture production company.